IN BEAUTY
IT IS FINISHED

Reflections on the Life and Work of Oliver La Farge

by Proal Heartwell

A publication of Lightfoot Press
In Beauty It Is Finished: Reflections on the Life and Work of Oliver La Farge by Proal Heartwell
Library of Congress Cataloging-in-Publication Data
ISBN 978-0-578-80494-1
BISAC: Biography & Autobiography; Native American Studies; Literary Criticism

Jacket photograph by Mullarky.
Colorized detail of "Best Dressed Navajos" with Oliver LaFarge,
Inter-Tribal Indian Ceremonial, Gallup, New Mexico, 1934.
Courtesy Palace of the Governors Photo Archives (NMHM/DCA), Negative Number: 134801

For the people of the Navajo Nation

and

In memory of Donovan Webster

PREFACE

Zing! Zup! Zing! Zup!

What was that noise? A man had just stepped outside the Jamestown palisade. He stopped in his tracks and looked quickly over his shoulder. He saw two arrows sticking in the side of the palisade. The Indians were after him, and he had left his gun in the fort. He started to run back and felt a sharp pain in his shoulder. An arrow had hit him. He stumbled over something. It was his hat. One of the Indians had shot it off and an arrow was sticking through the top of it. Somehow he got back to the fort alive.

So begins the third chapter of the Virginia history textbook I studied in the fourth grade. The year was 1964, 100 years after the Civil War, and I was growing up in a small town in Southside Virginia, less than 100 miles from Jamestown. As the fourth child of proud Virginians, I, of course, had already made the pilgrimage to Jamestown; the last leg of the journey required a ferry ride across the James River on the *Pocahontas*. I remember exploring the primitive settlement and going aboard the replica of the tiny *Susan Constant*, bobbing in the water alongside her sister ships, *Godspeed* and *Discovery*. Likely, I took note of the dugout canoe and the rudimentary tools found in the Indian village. My parents had no doubt made similar trips with my older siblings, and my mother and father had also traveled to the settlement in 1957, when a young Queen Elizabeth sojourned to Virginia to celebrate the 350th anniversary of the former colony's founding.

As a young boy, I was steeped in Virginia history, and I'm sure my pulse quickened reading the short staccato sentences of the passage above. I remember the textbook well: the gleaming cover whose lower half depicted the three-sided Jamestown Fort and whose upper half showed the three indomitable ships that carried the first Englishmen to the colony. The two images were bisected by large white script proclaiming the book's title: *Virginia's Story*. I did not think it remarkable that twenty-seven of the book's thirty chapters were required to tell the story of the 250 years from Virginia's founding to Lee's surrender at Appomattox. The remaining 100 years of the Commonwealth's history were quickly dispatched. Chapter 28 was titled "After the War Was Over," and Chapter 29 detailed "From 1900 Until Now." The last chapter was optimistically (and perhaps soberly) named "Virginia Looks to the Future."

My fourth grade year was the first that a handful of carefully chosen African-American children attended my small elementary school, a two-block walk from my home. Ten years after *Brown vs. the Board of Education*, Virginia tenaciously clung to the doctrine of "separate but equal" promulgated by the segregationist political machine headed by Democratic U.S. Senator Harry F. Byrd. The Byrd organization and other post-World War II leaders felt that Virginia children of that era were largely ignorant of Virginia history. The Second World War had ushered in a more mobile and transient society, and the veterans of that conflict, of course, had been exposed to a broader world and different ways of thinking. The Byrd Machine was also worried about the Civil Rights policies of the Truman Administration, and, according to a 2018 article in the *Richmond Times Dispatch*, Virginia's political leaders "wanted to tell a new generation of Virginians that Virginians were justified—in the mid-1800s and again in the mid-1900s—in wanting to handle race-related issues on their own." These leaders wanted to use the "Lost Cause" narrative of the Civil War to support ongoing segregation and keep meddling Northerners at bay.

Consequently, the Virginia History and Government Textbook Commission was convened in 1950 to oversee the creation of textbooks that conveyed the "Virginia Spirit." The Commission members included politicians, historians, and educators. They were responsible for reviewing the drafts of the texts, and they apparently took their job seriously, removing one lead author (born in Pennsylvania) for failing to adequately promote the party line. When published in 1957, the new books were widely defended. As one politician noted, "To explode the Pocahontas legend would be like saying there is no Santa Claus." (Much more on the "Pocahontas legend" in a bit.) The books were shipped across the state in 1957 and eventually found their way to Mrs. Mitchell's fourth grade classroom at Lawrenceville Elementary School. *The Washington Post* labeled these texts "more romance than history," and because of criticism in the 1960s about the books' depiction of slavery, they were phased out of use after the 1970 election of Linwood Holton, the first Republican governor of Virginia since Reconstruction.

During the 1950s and 60s, public school students in Virginia also studied the Commonwealth's history in seventh grade and eleventh grade. The seventh grade text produced by the Byrd Commission reassured the state's adolescent pupils that "a feeling of strong affection existed between masters and slaves in a majority of Virginia homes." This book also extolled the virtues of Robert E. Lee, widely considered a Virginian beyond reproach. Even his horse Traveler "stepped proudly, as if he knew that he carried a great general," the book noted. And the eleventh grade textbook, *Cavalier Commonwealth*, informed its readers that a slave "did not work so hard as the average free laborer, since he did not have to worry about losing his job."

As unenlightened as the Byrd Commission textbooks were, they are in some respects progressive when compared to the Virginia history books of the Jim Crow era. One such early work paints this idyllic portrait of antebellum quotidian life:

> Thomas Nelson Page says of those days: "I believe it was the purest and sweetest life ever lived. It gave the most to make this great nation. It led its armies and navies and made a strong government. It opened up the West and added Louisiana and Texas. This same social life brought Christ to the Negroes in less than two hundred years and a civilization which they had not known since the dawn of history. It made man noble, gentle, and brave and woman tender and true. It gave ideals and built faith in God and filled homes with purity and peace."

Of course, African-Americans might take exception to Page's contention that this time in history represented "the purest and sweetest life ever lived."

This same text describes plantation life thusly: "The little white boys played with their little brown body servants. They rolled over one another like little puppies." And, "always near the little [white] girls was to be found 'Mammy,' in charge of them. She sat on a near-by porch or in the shade of a tree and the youngest baby slept on her lap or toddled around her knees." These little girls, the book tells us, "had their own little maids" and these children played together with their dolls. Of course, the use of the word "servants" is indicative of the attitude of the times that produced this book, and you can almost hear Uncle Remus singing "Zippity-do-dah" in the background.

Chapter 40 of this text picks up Virginia history after the Civil War, or the "Late Unpleasantness" as my grandmother referred to the conflict. The chapter title, "Carrying On," suggests to me the heavy burden engendered by the South's defeat and particularly the fall of Virginia, the Cradle of the Confederacy. Commenting on the 1870 death of Robert E. Lee, the book eulogizes that "every heart in the South was sad. In death he was still followed—not as a dead hero, rather as a bright and living ideal, a shining star beckoning all to follow the light of his own noble life." Indeed, in the twentieth century the telling of Virginia history was inextricably linked to the life of Robert E. Lee, and it still is today. The textbook *School History of Virginia*, published in 1914, features a portrait of Lee on its title page. Certainly in my family, "Marse Robert" was regarded as a paragon of virtue, and any youthful transgression on my part might elicit "What would General Lee think?" from my parents or grandmother.

The memory of Robert E. Lee—and whether we should honor that memory—still informs contemporary society in Virginia. In August, 2017, white supremacists descended upon Charlottesville—where I have lived thirty-five years—ostensibly to protest a City Council vote to remove statues of Robert E. Lee and Stonewall Jackson from public parks. This protest devolved into a chaotic riot that resulted in three deaths. As of this writing the statues remain, although the names of their host parks—Lee and Jackson—have been changed. In 2019, a judge sided with plaintiffs in a suit against members of the City Council for their vote, ruling that the statues are deemed "war memorials" by state law and thus beyond the jurisdiction of local government. However, the 2020 Virginia General Assembly passed a bill granting local governments the authority to remove statues. That law has again been challenged in the courts and the litigation is ongoing.

Let me say that I unequivocally support removing these statues from public spaces. They were erected during the Jim Crow era, and they certainly can be viewed as symbols of oppression, then and now. In 1957, when he was writer-in-residence at the University of Virginia, William Faulkner was asked, "What of the Southern tradition and heritage do you hope [your grandson] will continue, and what do you hope [he] won't?" Faulkner responded, "I hope of course that he will cope with his environment as it changes. And I hope that his mother and father will try to raise him without bigotry as much as can be done. He can have a Confederate battle flag if he wants it, but he shouldn't take it too seriously." It seems to me, as Faulkner stated over sixty years ago, it is past time to cope with the changing environment.

So how did the textbooks of my youth (and earlier generations) depict American Indians? In Virginia's Racial Integrity Act of 1924 Native Americans were classified as Black and thus prohibited from interracial marriage. According to my seventh grade book, contact between English settlers and Virginia Indians created "a better life for both the settlers and the Indians." In a section titled "The Character of the Indian," that same book maintains that "War was the only method the Indians knew to settle disputes between tribes," and also that victorious warriors routinely "tortured their prisoners and burned them to death." However, as the book further states, "We must not forget that Powhatan and the people of his land had not yet learned the teachings of Christianity." On the same page, the reader is further reassured that the Indian was "capable of being a faithful friend." The 1914 *School History of Virginia* states that "[The native's] mode of living and constant warfare in which they were engaged rendered them cruel and revengeful, and they were extremely treacherous, but they would remember a kindness." I find it ironic that the authors of these two texts mollify their harsh characterizations by also acknowledging universal human virtues.

Our Virginia: A Description of Virginia for Young People was published in 1923. In his preface, author C. Ehrlich Smith writes, "Almost everybody in our state is American-born and American-bred. The early colonists of Virginia were the first Americans." I'm pretty sure that the indigenous Americans would take exception to Smith's claim. In a three-page overview of Indian life in Chapter One, Smith asserts, "Indians did not want very much—only guns, powder, whiskey and trinkets. The white men wanted the Indians' tobacco and the land on which they hunted." Seems simple enough, right? You give us your land and the means by which we may prosper, and we will give you that which will destroy your sovereign way of life. For as the officially sanctioned Byrd Commission eleventh grade textbook tells us, "The Indian's future was so uncertain that he lived for the moment. He seldom planned ahead. The lack of foresight made him less likely to anticipate the consequences of his acts. He fell into fury at slight insults and immediately started on the warpath unless he was restrained by a far-seeing chief."

Perhaps the Indian had justification for starting "on the warpath." In *The Story of Virginia* (1948), the first chapter summarizes life in the failed colony on Roanoke Island: "[The settlers] had trouble with the Indians. One day they missed a silver cup. Probably an Indian had taken it. To punish them, the whites burned an Indian village. This was a wicked act. It changed the friendly natives to enemies."

Let's return to the most enduring Native American story in Virginia history: the legend of Pocahontas. Chapter Three in *The Story of Virginia* is titled "An Indian King and a Princess." This chapter depicts Captain John Smith's first encounter with the young "princess":

> He [Smith] looked up and saw a small Indian girl standing on a fallen log. She looked like a graceful creature of the woods. She wore a doeskin skirt with shell beads and quills sewed all over it. She had copper bracelets on her brown arms. Her hair was black and straight, and very long. She was about ten or twelve years old and she had looked, unafraid, at the first white man she had ever seen.

This idyllic image could have indeed been the inspiration for Disney's animated portrait of Pocahontas from the eponymous film of 1995, and it is certainly in keeping with my own conception of the Indian maiden from my early schooling. In those years, of course, we all learned the story of how young Pocahontas saved the life of the intrepid Captain Smith, flinging her body over his prostrate form as her father, Chief Powhatan, prepared to execute the white man. And we fourth graders knew that Pocahontas's actions ushered in an era of relative good will between the colonists and "the red man." In *A History of Virginia for Boys and Girls* (1931), author John W. Wayland, Ph.D., concedes that this story is "probably true." He continues with, "Among the poets who have put it into verse was the great English writer, William Makepeace Thackery." Here is the last stanza of his poem:

> Dauntlessly aside she flings
> Lifted axe and thirsty knife.
> Fondly to his heart she clings
> And her bosom guards his life!
> In the woods of Powhatan,
> Still 'tis told by Indian fires
> How a daughter of their sires
> Saved a captive Englishman.

However, historian Karen Ordahl Kupperman suggests that this incident was perhaps an adoption ceremony. Smith was already known to Pocahontas, and to Powhatan, who wanted to symbolically strip him of his Englishness so he could be reborn as a member of the Chief's tribe. In fact, Pocahontas's impulsive act was actually carefully scripted so that Powhatan could use Smith to get goods he desired.

The young Pocahontas soon became a favorite at the fort in Jamestown, where she taught the English boys to cartwheel, but when she reached her maturity Powhatan arranged for her to marry Kocoum, a member of her tribe. As a schoolboy, I never knew that Pocahontas already had a husband when she wed the planter John Rolfe. Nor do I recall learning how she was captured by the English in 1613 and ransomed to her father for weapons, tools, and corn.

My Virginia history textbooks did tell the story of Pocahontas's conversion to Christianity and her subsequent marriage to John Rolfe. In

1614 she "renounced publicly her country's idolatry, openly confessed her Christian faith, [and] was, as she desired, baptized" and assumed the name Rebecca. John Rolfe played a crucial role in Pocahontas's conversion, feeling he was called by God to make her a Christian. During his voyage to Virginia in 1609, Rolfe was shipwrecked in Bermuda. He and others in his company, including his wife Sarah, made it to Virginia in 1610, but the couple's infant daughter, Bermuda, died on her namesake island; Sarah Rolfe died shortly after reaching Jamestown. John Rolfe was a devout man and sympathetic to the "heathens" who "bear the image of our heavenly creator, and we & they come from the same mold" for "what were we before the Gospel of Christ shined amongst us."

The marriage of Pocahontas and John Rolfe greatly benefited the colony of Virginia. She helped her husband produce a strain of tobacco that was sweeter and less noxious than previous crops and thus more palatable to English tastes. And, of course, Pocahontas's conversion to Christianity was a marketing boon to the Virginia Company, still seeking investors in England. In 1616, the Virginia Company brought the family (son Thomas Rolfe was born in 1615) to London, where Pocahontas took on the appearance of a Christian gentlewoman and was known as Lady Rebecca Rolfe. She was received at Court by Queen Elizabeth and visited by Captain John Smith, whom she declared she would call "father," insisting he should call her "child."

In the early spring of 1617, the Rolfe family prepared to return to Virginia, but Pocahontas died on board the ship on the Thames River, and was buried at St. George's Church at Gravesend on March 21, 1617. Rolfe and young Thomas sailed on, but stopped at Plymouth because Thomas was ill, and it was thought he might not survive the voyage to Virginia. He was sent to live with his uncle in Heacham and never saw his father again. John Rolfe arrived in Jamestown in mid-May, and in due time he married Joan Peirce, daughter of Captain William Peirce, who had been shipwrecked in Bermuda in 1609 with Rolfe and his first wife. John Rolfe died in an epidemic in 1623, and in 1635, Captain Peirce paid for the voyage to Virginia of the now grown Thomas Rolfe. Thomas married Jane Poythress and settled in Surrey County on lands left him by his father. Apparently, Thomas Rolfe had little or no contact with his mother's family.

The story of Pocahontas is indeed fascinating, and no wonder that it has captured the public imagination for so many years. As my fourth grade history textbook proclaimed, "Today in Virginia and in many parts of the United States, there are people who are descendants of John Rolfe and his wife, Princess Pocahontas." And I can attest to the fact that these descendants are extraordinarily proud of this lineage. Consider, for example, a wedding account of my wife's great-grandparents, the Reverend James Funsten of Richmond and Miss Ida Pratt of "Camden" in King George's County, Virginia, on November 23, 1886. A hyperbolic summary of the ceremony was published in the local paper the week following the nuptials. The write-up begins with an extensive description of the bride's home, the "beautiful mansion" Camden, where one can find "all that refined taste and luxurious habits could suggest, and that wealth can procure." Then follows a list of the bride's and groom's attendants, each described in glowing terms, including "Miss Gay Robertson, the beautiful brunette, simulating her kinswoman and prototype, the noble Pocahontas." Not to be outdone, the bride is referred to as "the golden prize— solid gold—whose beauty, freshness, brightness and purity stamp her as one of Virginia's bright jewels." Anyway, you get the picture. Interestingly enough, James Funsten eventually became the first Episcopal bishop of Idaho, where he ministered to many Native Americans. We have several photos of the Bishop in cohort with Indians in full tribal regalia.

And it seems that this sincere if somewhat misplaced pride would be the place where the Pocahontas story might end if not for Donald Trump and his need to coin disparaging nicknames for those who oppose him. Mr. Trump has a predilection for referring to Senator Elizabeth Warren of Massachusetts as "Pocahontas," a moniker he delivers in a derisive tone. After one such utterance, the *Charlottesville Daily Progress* responded in an editorial on October 22, 2018:

> If the Virginia General Assembly had any gumption, the next time it meets it would pass a resolution calling on Trump to stop calling Warren "Pocahontas." Not because we care about Warren—she has a Twitter account; she can take care of herself—but because we care about Pocahontas.

After the editorial traces Pocahontas's history, it concludes:

In mocking Warren as "Pocahontas," [Trump] takes her name
and turns it into an insult. If we Virginians still care about our history,
we shouldn't stand for that, no matter what our politics are.

Sadly, the Virginia General Assembly lacks gumption.

Approximately 100 years after the founding of Jamestown, Alexander
Spotswood was appointed Lieutenant Governor of Virginia, and he
immediately began efforts to improve relations with hostile Indians in the
royal colony. One of these efforts included building, in my native Brunswick
County, Fort Christanna. Named in honor of Christ and Queen Anne, the
fort was just "a musket shot" from a Sapponey Indian town. Within the fort
was a school, a chapel, and buildings necessary for the maintenance of the
garrison. Spotswood appointed the Reverend Charles Griffen as schoolmaster
at the fort, and thus began the first Christian Indian school in Virginia. At
one time, there were as many as seventy-seven Indian children being taught
at the fort, learning the "English tongue" so they might be able to read the
Bible and the Book of Common Prayer, and also learn to write. But "these
children were held as hostage, for it was felt that the treaty would be more
binding on the 'savages' since their children were at the fort." As we will see
later, there is a long and sad history in our country regarding Indian schools.
It seems likely that this history began in the pine forests along the banks of the
Meherrin River in Brunswick County, Virginia. (The school eventually moved
to Williamsburg and became part of the College of William and Mary.) As a
young boy, I accompanied my family on the occasional picnic on the former
grounds of Fort Christanna, and I delighted in finding arrowheads there. In
a local pamphlet published for the Jamestown Exposition, 1607–1907, the
author in fact writes:

Nearly every section of the county shows unmistakable traces of having been inhabited by Indians. It is quite a common occurrence for farmers while tilling their land to unearth arrow heads, tomahawks, and other implements of savage warfare, as well as occasionally the skull and bones of some deceased "brave" or "squaw," who has long hunted with bow and arrow, placed by his comrades in the grave, in the "happy hunting ground."

During my elementary school "indoctrination," I was also drawn to the story of Virginians Meriwether Lewis and William Clark, dispatched by President Thomas Jefferson to explore the unknown territory of the western United States acquired in the Louisiana Purchase. My comrades and I learned how these dauntless adventurers were aided in their journey by the young Shoshone woman, Sacagawea. Indeed, we understood that Sacagawea was instrumental to the expedition's success and the survival of its members. But now in Charlottesville another debate has emerged over art in public spaces. For 100 years Sacagawea has been depicted in a monument called "Their First View of the Pacific" on Charlottesville's West Main Street. In recent years, this statue has drawn criticism from some who interpret Sacagawea's crouching position as demeaning and one of subjugation to the standing figures of Lewis and Clark. Others, including members of the Shoshone tribe who visited the city in 2009, maintain that Sacagawea is tracking, thus cementing her role as an indispensable member of the expedition. However, the debate was settled in November, 2019, when Charlottesville City Council voted to direct city staff to create a plan for removing the statue. This action was taken after Council met with Native Americans, including some of Sacagawea's descendants. One of these descendants, Rose Ann Abrahamson, claims to have seen almost every depiction of her ancestor in the country and maintains that "This statue in Charlottesville was the worst we have ever seen." Her daughter added, "I can say for myself, it did bring shame. It made me feel sadness and worthlessness, and that's not how I was brought up."

And let's not forget William Clark's older brother, George Rogers Clark, the "Conqueror of the Northwest." A statue honoring Clark stands adjacent to the Grounds of the University of Virginia; recently, a petition circulated asking the school to remove the statue, which depicts an attack on a native family. After studying the sculpture and the history it depicts, a history that "celebrates genocide" according to one critic of the monument, the University decided on September 11, 2020, to remove the statue from the campus.

What else do I remember being taught about Native Americans in my youth? In those days, we students were often required to memorize and recite poetry, and I recall commiting to memory long chunks of Longfellow's "The Song of Hiawatha." ("On the shores of Gitche Gumee ...") I spent many Saturday mornings watching old TV Westerns where the wagons would circle to fend off attacks from scalping Indians. And I still recall the ridiculous sitcom "F Troop," which aired for two seasons during my preteen years. The show was set at Fort Courage in the years immediately after the Civil War, and one ongoing subplot featured the crooked schemes of the non-commissioned officers who acted in concert with the local Indian tribe—the Hekawis—led by Chief War Eagle. Played by Italian-American actor Frank de Kova, Chief War Eagle proclaims in one episode, "Don't let the name Wild Eagle fool you. I had it changed from Yellow Chicken." Needless to say, this show did little to disabuse me of my stereotypical views of Native Americans. And even my reading at the time reinforced these stereotypes. In Mark Twain's *The Adventures of Tom Sawyer*, Tom's friend Huck Finn refers to Injun' Joe as a "murderin' half-breed." Of course, throughout his writing career, Twain seemed to hold Native Americans in contempt. In *Roughing It*, he describes the fictional "Goshoot Indians" as "the wretchedest type of mankind I have ever seen ... inferior to all races of savages on our continent ... [They] were small, lean, 'scrawny' creatures; in complexion a dull black like the ordinary American negro." I now know that my attitude was one of ignorance and acceptance. As Oliver La Farge wrote in *The New York Times Magazine* in June, 1948, "Few white people understand an Indian or any of his motives. Most of them, in fact, see the stereotype, 'a befeathered, half-human creature of unnatural dignity with a habit of saying 'Ugh!'" And as Debby Irving points out in her memoir *Waking Up White*, the media of her childhood (and mine) reinforced La Farge's assessment: Native Americans were dangerous, especially when drunk.

One final observation on Indians from my adolescent years: I remember taking umbrage at the notion that the first Thanksgiving was celebrated in Massachusetts. Everyone knew, didn't they, that the real first Thanksgiving was held at Berkeley Plantation in Virginia, years before the Pilgrims and Squanto came up with the idea? Today writer Tommy Orange points out the irony of designating November, the month in which we celebrate Thanksgiving, as Native American Heritage Month. He acknowledges the strange juxtaposition of giving thanks for a people while also remembering the wrongs our ancestors committed against them. Furthermore, he questions whether we should continue to celebrate the holiday; perhaps, he suggests, we should use Thanksgiving as an occasion to talk about the true history of Native Americans.

When it was time for me to enter high school, my parents sent me to the all-male boarding school that my father and older brother had also attended. My years at Woodberry Forest School were positive and transformative. It was there that I learned how to be a student, and to approach my work with a certain diligence and sense of perseverance. I had many fine teachers at Woodberry, and I'm confident that their example inspired me to pursue teaching as a career. Some time during those four years at Woodberry, I first read *Laughing Boy*, Oliver La Farge's 1930 Pulitzer Prize winning novel. I'd like to say that this initial reading constitutes an epiphanic moment seared into my memory, that I can recall with clarity the specific time and place of my first encounter with the characters Laughing Boy and Slim Girl. But I can't, because that's not how memory—or at least my memory—works, because as we know, memory is a foreign country. As Patricia Hampl writes in *The Art of the Wasted Day*, memory is not a "transcription but ... an attempt ... to locate meaning between the irretrievable *then* and the equally unfathomable *now*."

So let's imagine that I was required to read *Laughing Boy* in my Fourth Form (10th grade) English class. I don't recollect a lot of particulars of that class, although I know with certainty that it was there that I first encountered

The Catcher in the Rye, a novel that changed my fifteen-year-old mind's conception of literature. I also remember that my teacher, Whitney Azoy, in a pique of anger and frustration, called one of my classmates "incorrigible," a word whose meaning I later had to look up in the library dictionary. And I obviously recall Mr. Azoy, a young and imposing figure with a full beard and a Harley-Davidson that he revved about the 1,000 acre campus and beyond. Mr Azoy left Woodberry after that year to join the State Department. Perhaps, he reasoned, foreign machinations might be less troublesome than a seething cauldron of 350 high school boys. I lost contact with Mr. Azoy after he left Woodberry, but a quick Google search of him takes me to the website of the Middle East Institute where I learn the following:

> Dr. Whitney Azoy has been involved with Afghanistan since 1971 as US diplomat, field anthropologist, refugee relief worker, scholarship director, reconstruction consultant, poetry translator, Pulitzer nominee journalist, National Geographic filmmaker, four-time Fulbright grantee, and Center Director for the American Institute of Afghanistan Studies in Kabul. He is currently coproducing a documentary film entitled "Afghanistan: A Nation of Poets."

Wow! I'd say my former English teacher made a wise career move. I also learn that Dr. Azoy is the author of *Buzkashi: Game and Power in Afghanistan*, a book that "is not only the first full-scale anthropological examination of a single sport, but also a beautifully written case study about a place and people that have been largely ignored in the social science literature." And just in case you are curious, apparently the game of Buzkashi "entails the aggressive struggle of hundreds of horsemen over a mutilated calf carcass." So, it makes sense to me that Mr. Azoy, with his interest in indigenous cultures and customs, would assign Oliver La Farge's *Laughing Boy*, a novel about the Navajo by a Harvard-trained anthropologist and ethnographer.

If my speculations are indeed correct, that year at Woodberry I was living in Taylor Hall, a utilitarian dormitory in the center of the campus. I can imagine myself sitting under one of the venerable oak trees on the grounds after lacrosse practice and before dinner, slowly turning the book's pages, absorbed in the doomed romance of the novel's protagonists. Or, perhaps, lying under the covers of my top bunk in the dim glow of a reading light while John, my roommate, snores below. I am intrigued by the portrait of Navajo life, so different from what I knew of Pocahontas and the Powhatans, yet presented in a manner that is easily understandable and palatable. Whatever my first experience of reading of *Laughing Boy* was, it is fair to say that this encounter changed my perception of Native American life.

Which brings us to the book in your hands. A few years ago, I read *Laughing Boy* again, the first time I had done so since my 1970s high school experience. And even though I discovered flaws in the novel that I either overlooked or didn't comprehend as a teenager, it is still, to my mind, a compelling and influential work. In a fit of nostalgic curiosity, I then began an obsessive examination of La Farge's life and writing: I read biographies and theses about La Farge, and I absorbed his canon of work, both fiction and nonfiction. I now hope to assess his life and work in the pages that follow because as one of his biographers notes, his life was a "study of paradoxes," and, as another critic writes, his "position ... in modern American fiction is a curious one."

I do not imagine my book to be necessarily a scholarly one, but more a synthesis or amalgamation of the literature by and about La Farge and my thoughts on this literature. The book is divided into four sections, each of which represents a major setting of La Farge's life: New England, New Orleans, New York, and New Mexico. It was my intention that each of the sections would also include reflections on my visits to these respective locales because, to again quote Patricia Hampl, "I almost never travel for a vacation—I take off on commemorative or even funerary experience, as if the world were a vast and not cheerless cemetery, the ghost still murmuring if you can get close enough." Such trips, Hampl notes, are "pilgrimages ... to the homes and haunts of figures ... who flared alive in my mind from reading." However, planned visits to Boston and Santa Fe in the spring of 2020 were derailed by the Covid 19 pandemic. Finally, in the book's afterword, I intend to provide a brief overview of Native American literature by examining a few seminal works of the genre.

So come along with me on this pilgrimage and let's see if we can hear "the ghost still murmuring," the ghost of the largely forgotten Oliver La Farge.

PART I: NEW ENGLAND

OLIVER LA FARGE ALWAYS THOUGHT OF HIMSELF AS A
Rhode Islander, a native son of New England, even though he was
born in New York City on December 19, 1901. And while he grew up and
attended primary school in that city, La Farge found comfort and meaning
in the family home in Saunderstown, Rhode Island, on the western shore of
Narragansett Bay. Oliver spent his summers and holidays at this house, where
he was part of a large contingent of adventurous and creative siblings and
cousins. It was a home where discussion was valued and reading encouraged;
Oliver, particularly, embraced reading and was known to work his way
through entire sets of encyclopedias. But the house and its environs afforded
the La Farge clan an expansive natural environment ready for exploration
and discovery. For example, it was here that Oliver learned to sail, a skill that
gave him confidence and proved to be an antidote to a certain clumsiness
that characterized his teenage years. As Oliver later writes in *Raw Material*,
a memoir comprised of a series of essays, it was "at the helm of [the nineteen
foot sloop] *Windingo* [that] I was altogether Oliver La Farge as he longed to
be, competent, sufficient, sure of himself." On the Narragansett Bay, La Farge
continues, "Imagination could still run free, but it did so less and less as
the all-sufficient occupation and endlessly changing beauty of sight, sound,
smell, and motion absorbed me. Here reality offered the absorption and self-
forgetfulness I sought eternally." In the same vignette, La Farge explains that
he and his siblings were encouraged to sail by their mother, who "was most
anxious to avoid building up fears in us, she wanted her children daring, and

so swallowed her own fears without a murmur" for "she hated a stuck-up boy as much as she did a coward."

Perhaps his mother's attitude had its genesis in the exploits of her own maternal great-grandfather, Oliver Hazard Perry, for whom Oliver Hazard Perry La Farge himself was named. Perry was an American naval hero in the War of 1812 when he defeated the British fleet on Lake Erie and famously proclaimed, "We have met the enemy and they are ours." For his actions in this decisive battle, Perry was awarded a Congressional Gold Medal, and a formal resolution of thanks from Congress. Perry died of yellow fever six years later at age thirty-four while on a government mission in Venezuela. Today there are many monuments in honor of Perry, including a statue outside the State House of his native Rhode Island.

Oliver's paternal great-grandfather was Jean-Frederic de La Farge, a former officer in the French army who took part in an 1802 expedition sent by Napoleon to quell a slave revolt in Saint Dominique, where he was captured by the insurgents. When the French withdrew in late 1803, de La Farge remained in the now independent country of Haiti before fleeing to Philadelphia in 1807 amidst rumors of a planned massacre of whites in the island nation. He then moved to New Orleans where his French connections helped him create a successful shipping and mercantile business. He became an American citizen (and Anglicized his name to La Farge), and in 1820 moved to Watertown, New York. There, La Farge bought properties popular with French exiles on the eastern shore of Lake Ontario. After marrying the daughter of a wealthy family who had fled their native France during the Revolution, La Farge eventually sold his holdings in upstate New York and moved to Manhattan, where he gained a fortune through his investments in commercial properties. He and his wife Louisa had nine children, including John La Farge, the esteemed American artist who was born in 1835.

An exploration of John La Farge on the internet reveals that he "is one of the most influential and important figures in the development of American painting," an artist of "great versatility" who worked with oils and watercolors on wood and on glass. He was "an artist of broad cultural interests" who has an "international reputation as a stained glass artist." And, La Farge's decoration of Trinity Church in Boston, according to the Smithsonian

American Art Museum, put him at the "forefront of the American Arts and Crafts movement."

John La Farge grew up in New York City and attended Mount Saint Mary's, a Roman Catholic College in Maryland before graduating from New York's St. John's College. In 1856 he traveled to Europe, where he briefly studied art in Paris. When he returned to the United States, he studied with William Morris Hunt in Newport, Rhode Island, and there he met his lifelong friends Willam and Henry James. In 1861 La Farge married Margaret Mason Perry, granddaughter of Oliver Hazard Perry and a great-granddaughter of Benjamin Franklin and Rebecca Mead. La Farge completed mural decorations for the aforementioned Trinity Church in Boston in 1876, and in 1887 he painted on canvas in place the "Ascension of Our Lord" above the altar of the Church of the Ascension in New York City. As an artist, La Farge admired the "formality and patterning" of Japanese art, and he made a trip to Japan with historian Henry Adams in 1886, an excursion that produced La Farge's book *An Artist's Letters from Japan* (1897). He also traveled to the South Seas, where he painted watercolors *en plein air*. According to the website of the Phillips Collection, these works feature "exotic subjects, spontaneous brush work, and delicately defined figures."

Today La Farge may best be remembered for his innovations and artistry with stained glass, as his work was commissioned by many churches, public buildings, and private residences, including the home of Cornelius Vanderbilt II. La Farge was the first artist to use opalescent glass, a stained glass medium he essentially invented. Apparently, La Farge introduced the material to young Louis Comfort Tiffany, but their once friendly relationship devolved into a decades-long acrimonious feud. The details of this feud and the resulting unsettled lawsuits are somewhat murky, but it seems that La Farge provided Tiffany with technical information and then the latter reneged on a promise to partner with La Farge.

John La Farge died in 1910. According to the website of the Smithsonian American Art Museum, he was a "cosmopolite" who "exercised a considerable personal magnetism" that drew many people to him, including his close friend, artist Winslow Homer. (When I was a boy, a print of Homer's painting "Breezing Up (A Fair Wind)" hung over my bed. It strikes me today that this rendering of a man and three boys sailing over a choppy body of water could represent Oliver, his brothers, Christopher and Francis, and their father, Grant aboard the *Windingo* on Narragansett Bay.)

On a recent trip to New York, my wife Susie and I—guided by our Brooklyn-based daughter, Elise—visited a few sites associated with John La Farge. Our first stop was the Brooklyn Museum of Art, where we had tickets to tour the fabulous Frida Kahlo exhibit then on display. Kahlo has always been a "family favorite," and Elise focused on the artist's life and work for a sophomore seminar project in high school. After meandering through the show and using the "Ask Brooklyn Museum" app, we were directed to two works of John La Farge, including the luminescent stained-glass piece, *Hospitalitas* (1906–07). The work's accompanying text read as follows:

> *Hospitalitas* was designed for the entrance hall stairwell landing of the Brooklyn house of Standard Oil head Herbert L. Pratt, which stood at 213 Clinton Avenue.
>
> The window is composed of the opalescent, or iridescent glass that revolutionized American stained glass at the end of the nineteenth century. Although debates continue as to whether the material was invented by the window's designer, John La Farge, or by his competitor, Louis Comfort Tiffany, it does seem certain that La Farge was the first to explore the medium.
>
> La Farge's earlier windows were often lush, Asian-inspired floral compositions in the Aesthetic Movement style. *Hospitalitas*, in which the main figure is dressed in classical garb and flanked by columns, may have been La Farge's attempt to reconcile his later art with the Neoclassicism of the then popular Beaux-Arts style.

I am intrigued by this citation and especially its reference to the ongoing debate regarding La Farge and Tiffany. While I'm a great admirer of Tiffany's work (my church in Charlottesville has several Tiffany windows), my allegiance to La Farge's story leads me to endorse him as the "inventor of the material."

It is raining hard as we leave the museum and hop on the subway to Greenwich Village and the Church of the Ascension on the corner of Fifth Avenue and West Tenth Street. I had previously emailed the church seeking permission to take pictures of the interior during the open hours for prayer, and that permission had been granted. Alas, two days before our departure for New York, when I called the Sexton to confirm our access, he informed me that the church would be closed that Friday for a wedding rehearsal. (I briefly consider—and then abandon—the idea of posing as an eccentric uncle and crashing the rehearsal.) Oh well. Nevertheless, we take photos of the exterior of the edifice and of the plaque affixed there. Among other things, we learn that this English Gothic church was built in 1840–41, and redesigned in "about" 1888 from plans by Stanford White, who also redesigned Thomas Jefferson's Rotunda on the grounds of the University of Virginia, my alma mater. (The Rotunda was restored to its original Jeffersonian design in 1976.) The plaque makes note of La Farge's mural and concludes by observing that President John Tyler (a Virginian!) married Julia Gardner at the Church on June 26, 1844.

We next head up Tenth Street, looking for the site of the building that once housed John La Farge's studio. We pass the apartment where La Farge's grandson Oliver first lived with his second wife, Consuelo Baca, before permanently relocating to New Mexico. We discover that the building that hosted John La Farge's workspace no longer exists. Instead, on the site is a large apartment complex, the Peter Warren. Peter Warren was a Vice Admiral in the British Royal Navy in the 18th century, and he acquired massive land holdings along the Atlantic coast, including hundreds of acres in what is now Greenwich Village. I pause to note the irony that a building named for Peter Warren has displaced the studio of John La Farge, whose wife's grandfather defeated the British navy on Lake Erie in 1813.

I later learn that the Tenth Street Studio, torn down in 1955, was once the most famous studio building in the United States. It housed several interconnected rooms off a central gallery, and among the artists who worked there were Frederic Edwin Church, Winslow Homer and, of course, John

La Farge, who "moved in before the plaster was dry." The building was the first substantial project of architect Richard Morris Hunt, brother of William Morris Hunt, John La Farge's early mentor in Newport, Rhode Island. Richard Morris Hunt enjoyed a distinguished career as a designer of many notable structures, including the entrance facade and Great Hall of the Metropolitan Museum of Art; the Biltmore estate, America's largest house located in Asheville, North Carolina; and many summer "cottages" in Newport. Hunt also designed the pedestal of the Statue of Liberty on Ellis Island. On this pedestal is Emma Lazarus's poem "The New Colossus," and during our trek that Friday, I discover that Lazurus lived on the same block that housed the Tenth Street Studio.

The next morning, a Saturday, our intrepid band continues its exploration, focusing on a couple of locations associated with Grant La Farge, John's eldest child and Oliver's father. Born in Newport on January 5, 1862, Christopher Grant La Farge studied architecture at the Massachusetts Institute of Technology, and married Florence Lockwood in Saunderstown in 1895. Professionally, La Farge partnered with George Lewis Heins, whom he met at M.I.T., and who married La Farge's aunt Aimée La Farge, John's youngest sister, who was only two years older than her nephew. The firm of Heins and La Farge was known for its design of church buildings, including the Fourth Presbyterian Church (now Annunciation Greek Orthodox Church) in the Upper West Side, and the Reformed Episcopal Church of the Reconciliation (now the Most Worshipful Enoch Grand Lodge of the Order of Masons) in the Bedford Stuyvesant neighborhood of Brooklyn. However, what became the firm's most prominent project—and our destination this day—is the Cathedral Church of St. John the Divine. Along the way to this edifice, we get off the train to take a photograph at the entrance of the subway station located at the intersection of 72nd Street, Broadway, and Amsterdam Avenue. This station was constructed in the early 1900s when Heins and La Farge were designing subway stations and buildings for the Interborough Rapid Transit Company. With its glass windows and gabled roof, this structure looks like a greenhouse or arboretum transplanted from a grand country estate. It is definitely the antithesis of the dark and dingy stairwells that characterize many Manhattan subway stops.

The Cathedral of St. John the Divine, situated between Amsterdam Avenue and Morningside Drive, looms imposingly above us as we approach it on foot along 112th Street. The Cathedral is touted as the world's largest Anglican Church, and it's certainly the biggest house of worship I've ever encountered. The exterior measures 601 feet by 232 feet, and the interior height of the nave is 124 feet; the Statue of Liberty—without its pedestal—would fit comfortably under the ceiling of the Cathedral. Before entering the structure, we pause to read the plaque fixed to its facade:

THIS EDIFICE SERVES THE EPISCOPAL CHURCH AS THE CATHEDRAL OF THE BISHOP OF NEW YORK. THE CORNERSTONE WAS LAID ON DECEMBER 27, 1892 AND THE FIRST SERVICE WAS HELD IN 1899 IN THE CRYPT BENEATH THE CHOIR. HEINS AND LA FARGE, THE ORIGINAL ARCHITECTS, WERE SUCCEEDED BY CRAM AND FERGUSON IN 1911 AND THEIR PRIOR ROMANESQUE PLANS WERE TRANSFORMED INTO A GOTHIC DESIGN.

As the plaque notes, construction of the Cathedral began in 1892, the year Ellis Island opened. Heins and La Farge completed the east end of the Crossing, but when Heins died in 1907, the trustees, preferring a more Gothic design, removed Grant La Farge from the project.

I grew up attending a small Episcopal church in rural Virginia, a church where on a good Sunday thirty congregants might gather to hear the Gospel. Needless to say, I am somewhat awestruck as I enter the nave of the Cathedral of St. John the Divine and gaze towards the altar, almost two football fields away. We explore the massive structure for the next hour, and from our perambulations and the Cathedral's official brochure, I note the following architectural tidbits:

- The Great Bronze doors are each 18 feet high, 6 feet wide, and weigh 3 tons. They were cast by Barbedienne of Paris, who also cast the Statue of Liberty.
- The 40-foot diameter Great Rose window in the West Facade, is

the largest in the United States and contains more than 10,000 pieces of glass.

- The 15th Century German choir stalls are on loan from the Metropolitan Museum of Art.
- The Nave features 14 themed bays honoring professions and human endeavor with stained glass windows that depict thematic scenes with religious and secular images.
- The 8,500 pipes of the Great Organ range from the size of a pencil to 32 feet tall.
- The figures bordering the entrance to the Chapels of Saint Saviour and Columba were sculpted by Gutzon Borglum, sculptor of the Mount Rushmore National Memorial.

Indeed, I am most attracted to the Chapels of Saint Saviour and Columba, designed by Heins and La Farge, and the five other chapels that fan out from behind the altar. Collectively known as the Chapels of the Tongues, these spaces were built in the early 1900s to commemorate the major immigrant groups that were then pouring into and building New York City. They vary in their design, and I find their intimate scale comforting and more in keeping with the physical scope of the worship experience of my youth. Each chapel "is dedicated to a different saint, corresponding to the patrons of Scandinavia, Germany, the British Isles, France, Italy, and Spain. The seventh [and first to be constructed], the Chapel of Saint Saviour is dedicated to the Christian communities of the global East."

The Chapel of Saint Saviour was dedicated in 1904 and measures 58 feet by 30½ feet. The twenty angels that flank the entrance and that were carved by Gutzon Borglum were modified from their original plaster casts, which depicted the angels as "decidedly feminine." Despite Borglum's contention that "In the angel idea there is something pure and spiritual and clearly beautiful which is more compatible with woman than man," complaints from clergy forced him to render the angels in a less "gender specific" manner.

My favorite chapel, however, is the Chapel of Saint Columba, also designed by Heins and La Farge and dedicated in 1911, the second of the chapels to be completed for worship. Measuring 50 feet by 27 feet, this chapel is named for one of the "foremost Celtic saints, and honors immigrants from Great Britain." The ten Borglum sculptures on each side of the Chapel entrance represent important British theologians. But for me, the most arresting aspect of this space is a bronze and white-gold triptych, created by Keith Haring, that rests on the altar table:

> This interpretation of the life of Christ is among the last works of noted New York City artist Keith Haring (1958–1990), completed just weeks before his death from AIDS. True to Haring's inimitable and exuberant style, the altarpiece is crowded with angels and human figures, whose outstretched limbs lead the eye to the central figure of Christ.

The piece has a beseeching and almost chaotic vibe about it, but the central radiant image of Christ welcoming all is full of grace and love. And my brief exposure to the Cathedral does suggest that such love remains at the core of its ministry. The brochure notes the Cathedral's many outreach programs and its vibrant and varied worship services including the annual Blessing of the Bicycles, which perhaps seems trivial until one realizes that twelve bike messengers were killed in the streets of New York in the first six months of 2019.

Despite his "removal" from the design and construction of the Cathedral of St. John the Divine, Grant La Farge enjoyed a prolific and accomplished career as an architect of, in particular, municipal buildings and university commissions, first in collaboration with Heins and later in his own practice after Heins's death. One such work that piques my interest is the partners' design of St. Anthony Hall—also known as Delta Psi fraternity—which stood from 1894 to 1913 at Yale University. Although the building no longer exists, the original gate adorns the current chapter house. St. Anthony Hall, founded at Columbia University in 1847, is a fraternity and literary society comprised of eleven active chapters. In addition to Columbia and Yale, St. A enclaves exist at Trinity College, Princeton University, Brown University, the University of North Carolina, the Massachusetts Institute of Technology, the University of Rochester, the University of Pennsylvania, the University of

Mississippi, and the University of Virginia; all but the last three are coed. I was a member of "The Hall" during my tenure at UVa in the mid 1970s, along with a contingent of classmates from Woodberry Forest School who joined ranks with young men from other largely Southern prep schools. I'm sure our chapter of St. A (Upsilon) was decidedly less "literary" than those of our northern brothers and sisters, and there was a great emphasis on drinking and partying at 133 Chancellor Street. It's safe to say we were fairly unenlightened when it came to matters of race (historian Thomas Nelson Page, quoted in the preface, was an early member of St. Anthony Hall at Virginia) and gender in what was then the infancy of integration and coeducation at "The University."

Indeed, I have very mixed feelings now—and I think I experienced some of these feelings as an undergraduate—when it comes to The Hall and fraternities in general. True, St. A offered me a comfortable place to live and eat, and I was surrounded by many bright and engaging friends, some of whom I am still close to today. Yet I confess to a certain unease when I reflect on some of the antediluvian attitudes I encountered and likely harbored. And I distinctly remember the disquietude I felt with "blackballing" prospective members who did not measure up to our self-perceived status.

Charles Dew teaches American history, the history of the South, and the history of the Civil War and Reconstruction at Williams College. A native of St. Petersburg, Florida, Dew attended Woodberry Forest School and Williams before earning his Ph.D. degree at Johns Hopkins University. He powerfully chronicles his upbringing and education in his 2016 memoir, *The Making of a Racist: A Southerner Reflects on Family, History, and the Slave Trade*. Dew recounts his lack of exposure to and attitudes about African Americans before he entered Williams College in September, 1954. There he encountered African American classmates and began to shed his racist indoctrination. During his undergraduate years, Dew belonged to St. Anthony Hall, which had an active chapter on campus at the time. In his memoir he describes a transformative moment he experienced at St. A during his senior year:

> The national Delta Psi officers were visiting, all adult men, and the national president was a Virginian, from Richmond. Since I was a Woodberry boy and he was a St. A from the UVa chapter, he assumed

he could speak frankly to me, and he drew me aside for a private conversation. "Charles, I hope the house here will have the good sense never to pledge a nigger," he said to me. I felt a knot form in the pit of my stomach and was flooded with a sense of anger and disgust. I had been taught since infancy to be polite around adults. But all that training meant nothing to me at that moment. I turned on my heels without saying a word and left the room.

I had finally broken free, really, totally free. Something had snapped in my education as a southerner, in my education as a racist. I was a different person from that Confederate youth, the born and bred southern white boy, the unthinking bigot who had stepped onto the Williams campus as a seventeen-year-old four years earlier.

One more note regarding Delta Psi: In 1920, Murry Falkner, treasurer of the University of Mississippi in Oxford, moved his family, including his son William Faulkner, recently returned home from service with the Canadian Royal Air Force in World War I, into the "old Delta Psi house, near the center of campus and almost a mile west of the [town] Square."

... the three-story structure was so solid and imposing that it reminded some of the old, ornate Geology Building. Three large, semicircular steps led up to the open marble terrace-like porch. An enormous arch set into the brick framed the double front door opening onto a large foyer. To the right was a huge many-paned set of three windows whose arched shape repeated that of the front entry. Five arched second-floor windows looked out on the front of the elm-shaded lawn, and set into the third floor below the peaked roof were three more windows. The most notable feature was a round tower attached to the front at the right. Rising to the top of the second story, it ended in a pointed conical roof which made it look like the donjon of a medieval castle. Murry and Maud Falkner had a downstairs bedroom. An old-fashioned circular stairway led to the second floor where the boys had their rooms. For a time Billy had a back bedroom upstairs; then he exchanged for the small room in the tower. Besides his bed and dresser there was a table where he worked at his manuscripts. The room also accommodated the supply of liquor he laid in whenever he could afford it. It was a spacious and comfortable house.

A group of young men built a clay tennis court in the yard, and the twenty-three-year-old William Faulkner fervently dedicated himself to mastering the sport before briefly relocating to New York City where by day he worked in a bookshop managed by Elizabeth Prall, later Mrs. Sherwood Anderson. He returned to Oxford and the Delta Psi house at the end of 1921, when he famously (or infamously) assumed the position of Postmaster and engaged himself in the literary and social life at Ole Miss. Faulkner was fired from his position in the fall of 1924, and after the publication of his book of poetry, *The Marble Faun*, he left for New Orleans in January, 1925. There he would reacquaint himself with Elizabeth Prall and, through her, meet Sherwood Anderson, and, as we shall see, befriend a young Harvard graduate named Oliver La Farge.

Although Grant La Farge's career was focused in metropolitan settings, he was a woodsman, hunter, and fisherman who tutored Oliver and his brothers in the out-of doors. As Oliver writes in *Raw Material*:

> A boy might be very much a pupil under instruction but at the same time my father let him feel he was an equal partner in the joint enterprise of hunting. There was a thrilling emotion to equality in a private world. All hunting was illuminated by his artist's response to beauty and his trained perception, which he knew very well how to convey. When the duck came, when a trout rose to the fly, when there was a hen grouse with her chicks in the springtime or a butterfly hovering in sunlight, he could pull you alert and into perception with his quiet voice. There was an eternally fresh excitement in his speech and his eyes.

Grant La Farge was a friend of Theodore Roosevelt's, and he designed and built the library at Roosevelt's home at Sagamore Hill. Both men shared a mutual affection for the West and were concerned about its preservation. Roosevelt trusted La Farge and consulted him on political matters, especially conservation issues. Grant La Farge knew much about different Indian tribes and their respective cultures, "from the Abenaki of eastern Canada to the Hopis of Arizona." As Oliver again writes:

> He had given me a little advice about getting on with Indians— go slow, be absolutely polite, observe every rule of good breeding, don't force talk, don't jabber, don't push yourself at them, never show surprise or lose your temper. All excellently true, and this, too, hinted at a challenge, at something difficult to do, perhaps requiring a special talent. My father thought so, and today I do, too.

In 1922, while Oliver was a student at Harvard, *American Indian Life* was published by the University of Nebraska Press. This anthology was edited by Elsie Crews Parsons and illustrated by Grant La Farge. In the preface to the book, Parsons writes that the work was conceived to educate the general reader about the life of the Indian. She expresses concern that tribal cultures disappear in America before people express interest in learning about them. Furthermore, she writes:

> In this book, the white man's traditions have been disregarded. That the writers have not read other traditions from their own culture into the culture they are describing is less certain. Try as we may, and it must be confessed that many of us do try very hard, few, if any of us, succeed in describing another culture, of ridding ourselves of our own cultural bias or habits of mind.

The writers of the anthology's twenty-seven stories are ethnologists, students, museum curators, and professors of anthropology including Oliver La Farge's then mentor, Alfred M. Tozzer, Professor of Anthropology at Harvard and the Curator of Middle American Archaeology at the Peabody Museum.

Each of the twenty-seven stories features a detailed pen and ink illustration by Grant La Farge, and his notes to these illustrations are appended to the book. For example, in describing his sketch for Alfred Tozzer's contribution, "The Toltec Architect of Chichen Itza," La Farge writes:

> Center, the stone ring through which, in the ball game, the ball was thrown. Background, a detail from the great colored frieze upon the interior walls of one of the temples. Sides, stone columns, representing the Plumed Serpent at either side of the Ball Court Temple. Alone, two conventional plumed serpents.

After the Depression began in 1929, Grant La Farge's business failed, and he returned to his Saunderstown home where he lived until his death in 1938. The house burned down in 1945, and the property was sold. Grant La Farge's artistic abilities and sensibilities—as well as those of his father John La Farge—proved to be an inspiration and a burden to Oliver. Throughout his young life, he questioned how best he could fulfill the artistic impulses so valued by his family. While he himself was a careful illustrator, Oliver La Farge determined that he would follow his muse through the medium of the written word.

Oliver's love and pursuit of writing were strongly encouraged by his mother, the former Florence Bayard Lockwood, member of a prominent family in American politics. Florence La Farge was a cultivated, artistic woman who deepened the social insights of her children. She encouraged them to "do their share," and she respected everyone who came to their house, "from ambassadors to the furnace man." She was friends to a number of influential and artistic people, including Owen Wister, author of the wildly popular novel, *The Virginian*. (Owen Wister served as a judge on the committee that awarded the 1930 Pulitzer Prize for Fiction to Oliver La Farge's *Laughing Boy*.) She oversaw the children's religious instruction, raising them as Episcopalians. Because of his dark black hair, slender frame, and easily tanned skin, Mrs. La Farge always called Oliver "Indian Man," and as long as she lived, he signed his letters to her "Thine Indian Man." Oliver routinely sent drafts of his writing to his mother, even after he was an established writer. She unfailingly encouraged him, yet did not hesitate to offer critical suggestions. It appears she remained Oliver's biggest fan until her death in 1944.

❧

Oliver La Farge's formal education began at St. Bernard's School, a primary school for boys initially located on Fifth Avenue in midtown in New York City before eventually settling at 4 East Ninety-eighth Street. Founded in 1904 by two Englishmen, St. Bernard's attracted students from upper class families with long associations in both the city and the nation. Oliver attended St. Bernard's from 1909 to 1914, and his older brother, Christopher, and his younger brother, Francis, also migrated through the school. Oliver found the atmosphere at St. Bernard's to be congenial and stimulating, much like his home environment where curiosity and inquiry were encouraged. He studied Latin at St. Bernard's, and his love of mythology flourished there.

A cursory review of *The Budget*, the school publication dating back to 1906, illuminates the character of the institution, its masters, and the boys who attended it. For example, we learn that *The Merchant of Venice* was "played by the boys of St. Bernard's School at The Berkeley Theatre, Christmas, 1910," and that the cast included the just-turned nine-year-old Oliver H. P. La Farge as Jessica, daughter of Shylock. (Oliver's older brother, Christopher, portrayed Antonio in the production.) As *The Budget* reports, "It was 'vaulting ambition' to present a Shakespearean comedy without cut with a cast composed of boys under fourteen years of age. But the result proved it was worthwhile to risk the fall." Furthermore, "the performance itself was distinctly credible. The boys knew their parts well and spoke the lines naturally and intelligently."

A 1913 edition of the publication announces that "the School Play will take place at the Berkeley Theatre as usual on Friday, December the 12th." Furthermore, "the Prologue which reads as follows, will be spoken by John Hay Whitney":

> Oyez, Oyez, Oyez,
> I am the Prologue to the Play.

And I speak my speech and I make my bow
For love of the days gone by, I trow
With his jolly gifts and his customs quaint,
And I whisper a welcome warm and wide
To the bells of a Merry Christmastide.

I speak in the name of my schoolmates here,
When I wish you joy in the coming year,
When I crave your kindliest thoughts to-night,
For a play that is played for your true delight.

Good night, good friends, I would gladly stay;
But the scene is set and the play must play;
The scene is set and the prompter calls—
Let us all be boys until the curtain falls!

Of course, we don't know how well nine-year-old John Hay (Jock) Whitney delivered this prologue, but his February 9, 1982 obituary in *The New York Times* relates that he "stuttered and lisped as a small boy, but he conquered both afflictions in later years." The Whitneys were a wealthy and distinguished family, and Jock's maternal grandfather, John Hay, was secretary to President Lincoln and Ambassador to Britain and Secretary of State under Presidents William McKinley and Theodore Roosevelt. His paternal grandfather, William C. Whitney, was Secretary of the Navy in the administration of President Grover Cleveland. Like the La Farge brothers, Whitney went from St. Bernard's to Groton before he (unlike the La Farges) matriculated at Yale. Whitney enjoyed great wealth and was a noted philanthropist. A bridge and golfing partner of President Dwight D. Eisenhower, he was Ambassador to Britain from 1957 to 1961. Whitney was also known for his extensive art collection, which included works by Rembrandt, Michelangelo, Picasso, Monet, Cezanne, and others.

The Budget goes on to report that after the school play, two pieces by W. S. Gilbert are to be performed. The second of these is a "jolly farce, 'Creatures of Impulse,'" and the cast includes Oliver H. P. La Farge as "A Strange Old

Lady." (Apparently, La Farge carried off his part well. In the April 1914 edition of *The Budget*, "Creatures of Impulse" is reviewed, and the critic notes that "Oliver La Farge, looking like the Witch of Endor, cursed most dramatically.") *The Budget* provides the following overview under the heading of "Entertainment" in the earlier 1913 edition:

> There have been no lectures this term. Our old friends had been heard so often and our new lectures were so feeble that we thought a year's rest might be advisable.
>
> Instead we hope to have some entertainment, which, if not instructive, will, at least, be amusing.
>
> The first of these was given on Thursday afternoon, December the 4th.
>
> The boys assembled in the schoolroom and half past four arrived. There was no sign of Major Horsfield, who had most kindly promised to show some card tricks and sing some songs.
>
> So Mr. Jenkins sat down to the piano and the boys sang, or rather "shouted" "John Brown's Body," "The Wild Man of Borneo," and such familiar ditties.
>
> At last Major Horsfield arrived and mounted on a table. He called for an assistant and proceeded to show how certain card tricks were done. It was difficult to make the seething audience see these properly, so Major Horsfield sat down to the piano and gave a musical sketch.
>
> The laughter was so great that any ordinary entertainer would have been nonplussed, but Major Horsfield seemed to enjoy it as much as the boys and only played and sang louder than ever.

But Oliver was also active in other realms of school life. He played forward on the soccer team, but after a November 24, 1913, 3–0 loss to Riverdale School at Van Cortlandt Park, *The Budget* noted that "the forwards, as a whole, showed very little combination and were lacking in energy."

Even the students' grades seem to have been published in *The Budget*. A list of marks from 1912 includes "La Farge, II—Spelling, 75." (At St. Bernard's, Oliver was always referred to as "La Farge, II" so as to distinguish him from his older brother Christopher, "La Farge, I.")

Oliver's experiences at St. Bernard's were instrumental in his intellectual and emotional growth. He reveled in the conviviality and scholarship of the school, where he honed his inquisitive nature and nurtured the habits of mind that abetted his life of research and discovery.

In the fall of 1914 Oliver La Farge followed his older brother, Christopher, to Groton, an elite all-male boarding school in Groton, Massachusetts, where he would spend the next several years in a state of adolescent angst. Groton School was founded in 1884 by twenty-seven-year-old Reverend Endicott Peabody on land along the Nashua River with views of the distant mountains of Wachusett. Elements of its central campus were designed by landscape architect Frederick Law Olmstead, who also designed Central Park and Boston Public Garden. Franklin Roosevelt was an early graduate of Groton, and Theodore Roosevelt sent his four sons there. Oliver was largely unhappy at Groton, which he considered to be a "totalitarian community." As he recalls in *Raw Material*, thirty years after his graduation,

> At Groton it was important to be regular. There were certain types of conspicuousness which were admirable, they fitted the general pattern and had long been prescribed. Apart from them, inconspicuousness, regularity, was to be sought. The collection of negatives and positives which govern our behaviour, the many precepts expressed to us, all served to sketch out a fairly explicit and detailed ideal—the Groton Boy.

According to La Farge, the "Groton Boy" is one for whom intellectual capacity is of secondary importance. Furthermore, he should be a conformist with no strong aesthetic leanings. However, he should at all times be courageous and honorable.

As one of his schoolmates recounted, La Farge was an individualist in an environment that discouraged nonconformity. In many ways, Groton seemed to stress values that were antithetical to La Farge's upbringing and his education at St. Bernard's, where curiosity was encouraged. At Groton, according to La Farge,

> One needed to be circumspect. The *tone* of the school, that indefinable, all dominant thing, standardized acceptable behavior in ways that went beyond rules, regulations, and good manners. An artist was bound to offend, so was any sensitive, strongly reacting person, any natural intellectual with a probing mind and an emotional love of truth.

Peter Brooks is a Managing Director and Co-Founder of CornerStone Partners LLC, a Charlottesville-based investment firm. I taught both of Peter's daughters in middle school, and like Oliver La Farge, Peter attended St. Bernard's, Groton, and Harvard. And like La Farge, Peter harbors fond memories of St. Bernard's, steeped in British public school tradition. As a boy, he considered St. Bernard's "very academic," and a place where it was important to play a sport and learn school songs. According to Peter, the St. Bernard's/Groton path was a "well trodden" one, and St. Bernard's graduates were well-prepared and a "notch above" upon entering Groton. When, over a cup of coffee, Peter and I discussed the life of Oliver La Farge, Peter was not surprised to learn of La Farge's unhappiness at Groton, where it was important to be a "manly Christian." Peter's own Groton experience was a positive one; still, he recalls how even in 1965 when he entered the school, there was little hot water or heat in the dormitories and no doors on the students' rooms. Peter remembers that at Groton there was sparse down time and thinks the non-contemplative atmosphere would have been challenging for a student like La Farge who was sensitive to his own inadequacies.

Still, Oliver was not entirely unhappy at Groton. He committed himself to writing, and he enjoyed some success playing football, high jumping, and rowing. At Groton, La Farge discovered an interest in anthropology when, during his fourth-form year, his mother sent her fifteen-year-old son a book review by Teddy Roosevelt of *Men of the Old Stone Age* by Henry Fairfield Osborne, another La Farge family friend. La Farge was fascinated by the book;

perhaps, he considered, he could somehow combine his love of writing with the art of social science.

As an adolescent boy, Groton held a mythical spot in my imagination. While I knew I was destined for Woodberry Forest, the alma mater of my father and brother, I was nonetheless intrigued by the Groton of my mind's eye. An older first cousin had matriculated at Groton, traveling there all the way from Alabama, where his mother and my own had grown up together as sisters. A few years later, this cousin's younger brother followed him to Massachusetts. I am essentially the same age as this younger brother, and we are both named after our maternal ancestors. My second year at Woodberry Forest, a new headmaster assumed the reins at our school. The Reverend Charles Sheerin, a native Virginian, came from Groton, where he had served as chaplain, to lead Woodberry. Sheerin brought with him a librarian and an English teacher, both experienced masters at Groton.

During my junior year, Groton and Woodberry initiated an exchange program. My memory has dimmed as to the particulars of this effort, but I do recall befriending Andy Woolworth, a Groton student with a decidedly Groton last name, I thought, who spent a trimester at our campus in rural Virginia. I was eager to participate in this fledgling program the next year; I thought it would be fun to experience something new and hang out with my cousin. Alas, it was not to be. As I wrote in a fit of hubris to my parents,

> Groton is looking pretty slim. The boys who want to come down here are not worthy in Mr. Sheerin's esteem. He told Mr. Wright [the Groton headmaster] to find two boys as good as French and I, but that would seem impossible.

Sorry, cuz! It seemed I was destined to visit Groton only in my mind.

Oliver La Farge followed the natural academic pipeline from Groton to Harvard in the fall of 1920. Of Harvard he wrote, "[It] was my release and great happiness. There I knew success, prominence, my first true friendships, and real joy of the mind." He quickly involved himself in campus life. He began rowing as a fifth former at Groton, and he continued the sport at Harvard. He joined the *Advocate*, the school's literary journal, and published thirty-four pieces in the magazine over the next four years. He was a member of the Harvard Student Council and on the editorial staff of the *Lampoon*, and he was chosen by his peers as the official poet of the Class of 1924.

However, La Farge also experienced disappointment when he was not initially accepted into one of the social clubs at the advent of his sophomore year. He wrote his mother, "There is something wrong with your son, somewhere, and I wish I could spot it." His insecurity was fueled by the fact that many cousins and family friends were members of the very clubs to which he aspired, yet he received no bids. Eventually, in his junior year, La Farge was accepted into two clubs, but still deeply felt the wound of his earlier rejection.

In his essay "The Eight-Oared Shell" (1942), La Farge writes, "Rowing at School [Groton] was fun, but rowing at Harvard was magnificent." For La Farge, "rowing became … an occupation, something complete in itself in which I entered and from which I returned to ordinary life, it maintained its own, unbroken stream winding through the outer currents of my existence." La Farge was a member of the first 150-pound varsity crew at Harvard, where he manned the five oar "which is, with six, the driving position deluxe." He reveled in the beauty and precision of the sport and clearly delighted in the camaraderie it afforded. He describes the immediate aftermath of a race in the following passage:

> You have known complete exertion, you have answered every trouble of mind, spirit, and being with skilled violence and guided unrestraint, a complete happiness with eight other men over a short stretch of water has brought you catharsis. You may find it in storms at sea, in the presence of your art, on a racing horse, in bed with a woman, but you will hardly find it better or purer than you found it here.

As mentioned before, La Farge wrote prolifically at Harvard. His pieces for the *Advocate* were varied in scope, and they suggested new interests and fields of possibility. He began to earnestly think of himself as a writer, and became increasingly confident of his ability. He believed he had the requisite talent, and he knew he had the desire and drive to mine that talent and polish his craft.

La Farge declared anthropology as his major at Harvard, perhaps because of the influence of his father and the publication of the illustrated *American Indian Life* in 1922 during his sophomore year. Or perhaps his decision to study anthropology was born from his enthusiasm for *Men of the Old Stone Age*, the book by family friend Henry Fairfield Osborne that his mother sent Oliver when he was a student at Groton. During his tenure at Harvard, La Farge participated in three expeditions to the American Southwest, the first taking place in 1921 when he was nineteen years old. Since the 1880s, Harvard had been sending students to the Southwest, where aspiring anthropologists could learn practical tricks of the trade. Archaeology in America was in its infancy in the 1920s and the field was not heavily populated. La Farge and his fellow students were commissioned to explore whether or not the Southwest was occupied by humankind before the epoch of the cliff dwelling people of Mesa Verde and similar sites.

Apparently La Farge had little initial interest in this question. He would have preferred exploring Stone Age caves in France. But at the prompting of Dr. Alfred Tozzer, director of Harvard's Division of Anthropology, La Farge soon found himself in a landscape he called "a howling ash-heap," where horseback riding "was a pain in the neck." He was disoriented by this alien environment, and his first encounters with the Navajo were oddly unsettling; as he described them they were "a strange people, impenetrable to all appearance, yet behind the mask of race there lay a humanity one longed to explore." Soon he fell under the spell of the Navajo, later admitting, "The Indians had got me." However, he determined he would not be an archaeologist, but rather immerse himself in the life of the Navajo tribe. As he wrote in *Raw Material*:

> The men of the Old Stone Age in France disappeared from mind, archaeology was a comparatively dull occupation ... and in the end I should become an ethnologist—specializing, of course, in the Navajo Indians. There would come a day, at the end of a great number of utterly delightful days of desert camping and horseback, when I would

sit at ease in their hogans, speaking the language, wearing the costume, accepted, perhaps, adopted into the tribe.

Back at Harvard, determined to understand the beliefs, customs, and literature of the Navajo people, La Farge explored materials in the Peabody Museum. They appealed to his scientific intellect while also engaging his writer's imagination, and he wondered if he could forge a career from these interests. La Farge made two more expeditions to the Southwest during his years at Harvard, and he was, in fact, the expedition leader in the 1924 exploration, a trip that culminated for La Farge in a 140-mile journey on horseback to the Grand Canyon. During this excursion he experienced much hospitality from the Navajo, and their acts of kindness cemented the connection he felt for them and their heritage.

I have visited Harvard twice in my life, first when I was a senior at Woodberry and in the midst of the college application process. I traveled there with my friend Hervey on a school-sanctioned college visitation weekend. After a Friday football game at St. Christopher's School in Richmond, Hervey and I caught a ride to Washington and from there took the train to Boston. Hervey's brother Rob, a Woodberry graduate, was then a student at Harvard, and I'm assuming we slept on the floor of his dorm room. The next day, we attended the Harvard-Dartmouth game in Cambridge; the plan was then to hitchhike to Dartmouth after the contest. Surely there would be Dartmouth students returning to their campus, eager to give a ride to two earnest young men. Well, the only ride that materialized that cold, sleety late afternoon was a Massachusetts state trooper who took pity on us because we were from Virginia, where he had once been the governor's chauffeur. The officer took us to some small town and dropped us off at a hotel where he knew we could get a room for $3.00. Before driving away, he told us—in no uncertain terms—to be on the 7:00 a.m. bus the next morning for Hanover, New Hampshire. We were.

After spending the day at Dartmouth (There was a soft-serve ice cream machine in the cafeteria!), Hervey and I somehow (another bus?) traveled to Williamstown, Massachusetts, to visit Williams College. There, we both had formal interviews with admissions' officers before rendezvousing with another Woodberry classmate who showed up with his old Jeep Cherokee.

The three of us took shifts driving back to Virginia, arriving at Woodberry at 2:00 a. m. Tuesday.

Needless to say, I don't remember much about my whirlwind tour of Harvard; I can't even recall who won the football game. My only memory is the frustration of Hervey's brother over the results of a poll sponsored by the campus radio station. When asked to pick the greatest rock song ever, the students at Harvard chose "Maggie May" by Rod Stewart and Faces over the Beatles' "Hey Jude." I understood then—and I understand now—Rob's disappointment in the musical tastes of his fellow Crimson.

My second visit to Harvard came in 2016 at the invitation of The International Conference on Welsh Studies, where I delivered a paper titled "Goronwy Owen: A Welsh Poet Exiled in Virginia." I had previously written a book about Owen, an eighteenth-century poet who is still today much revered in his native Wales. Owen was also an Anglican clergyman, who came to Virginia in the late 1750s to teach Latin and Greek at the College of William and Mary, where Thomas Jefferson numbered among his pupils. Owen's tenure at the College was a brief one, as he was essentially forced to resign his position due to his bad behavior. He spent the remaining years of his life as rector of St. Andrew's Parish in rural Brunswick County, Virginia.

The International Conference on Welsh Studies is a biennial affair, and its last incarnation before the Harvard gathering had been in Cardiff. Approximately 100 people attended the Harvard conference, a week-long examination and celebration of Welsh history, literature, and culture. Most of the attendees were from Welsh universities, and the panel discussions were full-on immersion into Welsh esoterica. My wife, Susie, accompanied me on this trip, and of course we attended many of the events associated with the conference. But we also used our time in Boston to explore the city's historic attractions, and we even took in a baseball game at Fenway Park. We also made a quick sojourn to Concord to visit the homes of some of my literary heroes: Ralph Waldo Emerson, Henry David Thoreau, and Louisa May Alcott.

On our first day at Harvard, Susie and I marched out to the center of a bridge spanning the Charles River, the bridge where Quentin Compson plunged to his death in *The Sound and the Fury*. In the days that followed, we absorbed the sights and sounds of the campus, including the Widener Library, and I recall our amusement and astonishment when one afternoon we spied a turkey—yes, a turkey—sauntering down the middle of Massachusetts Avenue.

At the time of this trip I was not yet engaged in La Farge mania, but looking back on that visit, I can easily picture young Oliver writing a story in the offices of the Harvard *Advocate*, perusing Native American artifacts at the Peabody Museum, or manning the number five oar of an eight-oared shell gliding down the Charles River.

La Farge returned to Harvard in the fall of 1924 to begin graduate study on the Navajo as a Hemenway fellow. The Hemenway fellowship was named after Mary Tileston Hemenway (1820–1894), great-grandmother of my friend, Charlottesville attorney Michael Hemenway. A Massachusetts socialite and philanthropist, Mary Hemenway supported a number of educational and historical projects after the Civil War, including the Hemenway Southwestern Archaeological Expedition which took place between 1886 and 1894. The expedition's purpose was to conduct archaeological and anthropological forays in New Mexico and Arizona, and several reports of the expedition's findings were subsequently published. In 1895 the Hemenway family donated a box of expedition artifacts to Harvard's Peabody Museum of Archaeology and Ethnology. For whatever reason, the box remained unopened until the 1930s when Alfred Tozzer asked one of his students to explore its contents and write a dissertation on them. And it was not until 100 years after the Hemenway Expedition that a full three-volume report of the project was published.

In 1878, Mary Hemenway made a gift of 350 acres on the Back River in Virginia to Hampton Institute, four and a half miles from the donated land. This tract eventually grew to more than 600 acres, and its history is detailed in the September 1892 edition of *The Southern Workman and Hampton School Record*, a publication that reports "work for and progress of the Black and Red Races of our country." The sixteen-page monthly bulletin, which cost one dollar a year, is "Printed on the Normal School Steam Press by Negro and Indian students trained in the office." At the Hemenway Farm, the journal claims, "the boys are all on wages. They earn about ten dollars a month apiece, besides board, which is saved up to pay future school bills for board and clothing." The boys study at night to "master the simplest English elements" and to prepare to enter the Normal (teacher training) School. "Clean living, good behavior, character and skill are the best and well proved results of the Hemenway Farm in the past fourteen years."

As the bulletin's statement of purpose also declares, "Each number contains a broadside of letters from this school's 723 graduates who have, since 1868, taught 129,475 children in over twelve states in the South and West. Furthermore,

> With these direct reports from the heart of Negro and Indian populations are pictures of Reservation, Cabin, and Plantation life, and Local Sketches; a running account of what is going on in the Hampton School with its thousand souls in all departments, in which sixteen branches of industry are taught; press clippings showing the trend of public sentiment on both race questions; original thoughts of the nation's young wards as they emerge from ignorance into light and larger views; and editorial comment.

It's clear that the avowed purpose of the *Southern Workman* is to present the accomplishments accrued by the "Black and Red Races" from their education at the Normal School. Northern subscribers to the *Southern Workman* are encouraged to support the school's mission with "charitable investments," and the many testimonials found within its pages bear witness to the fruits of such contributions.

In 1884 the Indian Rights Association of Philadelphia published the report of a trip "To Some Indian Reservations of the Southwest by S. C. Armstrong, Principal of Hampton School, Va." Of the Navajo Indians of Northern New Mexico, Armstrong writes, "They now face a prospect of the care and attention that shall greatly improve their condition." He further reports that

They have always lived as they are, but the pressure of white men's enterprise, which is advancing on every side, may ere long create a crisis, for they can hardly support their million sheep and their twenty-six thousand ponies on their riverless reservation, where, with vast grazing land, there is very little water, and but few acres near springs that are arable.

Besides schooling for their children, in which their interest has just been aroused, they need practical instruction that could only be given by a corps of assistant farmers who should develop their water resources, introduce new farming utensils, seed, and blooded stock of every kind, improving their wool, the annual clip of which is even now very large, also the miserable huts they live in; and, finally, make them a wealth-producing class in the Southwest.

Armstrong goes on to detail existing conditions in over a dozen other tribes of the Southwest before concluding that "Whatever is essential to the manhood and civilization of the Indian is supplied by Congress with parsimony unaccountable except from ignorance or indifference." Armstrong warns that unless the "Indian question" is honestly confronted, the "red race" will be a national disgrace. He closes his report with a statement of important points to address the Indian question. These points include manual labor training for Indians of school age, instruction in practical farming for the current generation of Indian men and women, making Indians U.S. citizens as quickly as possible, providing adequate salaries for Indian agents, and creating funds to police the sale of liquor to Indians. As Armstrong writes, "Rum is the red man's greatest danger."

As a Virginian, I'm chagrined to admit I never knew about the connection between Hampton Institute, founded in 1868, and the well-intentioned but perhaps ill-conceived education of Native American children between 1878 and 1923. Because of Virginians' predilection to claim kinship with Pocahontas, it was hoped that the presence of Indian students would mitigate locals' unease about educating African-Americans in the aftermath of the Civil War. But in 1923 the program was suspended because of concerns over racial mingling. When employees started firing Native Americans because they had been educated with Blacks, Indians stopped sending their children to the school.

La Farge's graduate work as a Hemenway fellow was abruptly interrupted mid-year, and he did not complete his masters' thesis until 1929. The cause of this hiatus was an offer from Frans Blom, a young anthropologist La Farge had met during his last undergraduate year at Harvard. Blom was commissioned to hire a junior member for the Carnegie Institute field program, and he offered the position to La Farge just before La Farge left on the 1924 Navajo expedition. Oliver accepted the offer, but the Carnegie trip to Central America was suddenly cancelled. However, Blom, who was associated with Tulane University and who created there the Department of Middle American Research, secured funding for the proposed expedition. Blom asked La Farge to accompany him on the Department's first field exploration, and Oliver left Harvard in the fall of 1925 and joined Blom in Mexico City as the pair embarked on a five-month-long journey through the Mayan country of Mexico and Guatemala.

La Farge returned to Harvard after the trip, but in 1926 he officially joined the Department of Middle American Research at Tulane as an assistant in ethnology. Just twenty-seven years-old at the time, he spent the next two-and-a-half years in New Orleans, where he also began his career as a professional writer, and where he would largely compose his defining work.

PART II: NEW ORLEANS

F RANS BLOM LED A PERIPATETIC AND ADVENTUROUS LIFE
before joining Tulane's Department of Middle American Research in
1924. A native of Denmark, a gifted linguist, and just a few years older than
Oliver La Farge, Blom had worked for an oil company in southern Mexico
in 1919, and had developed an interest in Mayan ruins. He changed careers
to pursue archaeology with the Carnegie Institution and eventually enrolled
in Alfred Tozzer's class in Mayan archaeology and hieroglyphics at Harvard,
where he met La Farge.

As previously mentioned, La Farge joined Blom in Mexico City in
March, 1925, on "an expedition to middle America [Mexico and Guatemala]
conducted by The Tulane University of Louisiana." This expedition, which
eventually covered 1,200 miles, led to the publication in 1926 of the two-
volume *Tribes and Temples*. The preface of the book begins thusly:

> In March, 1924, an anonymous friend of Tulane University
> created an endowment, the income from which would be used for
> the study of the Middle American countries. It was then decided to
> conduct an archaeological and ethnological investigation through
> library research and expeditions to be sent into the fields formerly
> inhabited by the most notable of the ancient population of America,
> the Maya Indians.
>
> Mr. Frans Blom was selected to take charge of the first expedition,
> assisted by Mr. Oliver La Farge. They started from New Orleans on

the 19th of February, 1925. [La Farge did not join Blom for several days when he met him in Mexico City.] The object of the expedition was to study the ancient remains, as well as the customs and languages of the Indians. At the same time notes were taken on various other subjects.

The work was so distributed that Mr. Blom made studies of everything pertaining to archaeology and he also collected geographic data. Mr. La Farge gathered material relating to the customs and languages of the present day Indians.

The preface goes on to point out that the form of the book, based on the authors' journals, is that of a travel book that can be appreciated by the general reader as well as the scientist. It is noted that "the sections on archaeology have been written by Mr. Blom and those parts relating to present-day Indians, by Mr. La Farge." I borrowed a copy of *Tribes and Temples* from Alderman Library at the University of Virginia, and the volume's flyleaf was inscribed "With the Compliments of Dr. A. B. Dinwiddie," President of Tulane University. Dr. Dinwiddie was a graduate of the University of Virginia, and he would play an important role in Oliver La Farge's brief tenure in New Orleans.

I found that *Tribes and Temples* did appeal to me, "the general reader." The text is compelling and informative ("No member of such an expedition should ever be without a compass, a snake bite pencil, and an army emergency ration"), and the narrative's tone is often understated and satirical ("It was quite cheerful to hear that we had made no progress during the last hour's ride"). The book relates anecdotal information such as the relationship between chewing gum and Mayan archaeology, and it clearly details dramatic moments, as when the authors save the life of an Indian boy bitten by a venomous snake. Excavations are precisely recorded, as are the interactions between expedition members and local indigenous people. Throughout the narrative there are careful pen and ink drawings by La Farge on everything from ruins to worship ceremonies to regional flora and fauna.

The epilogue contains the usual "thank yous" to supporting institutions and people, especially "Lazaro Hernandez Guillermo, our guide and friend, whose broad shoulders carried their share of the burdens." Interestingly enough, Lazaro Hernandez Guillermo, or "Tata" as the authors called him returned to New Orleans with Blom and La Farge, and he became a familiar sight in the French Quarter. The epilogue also states that

> It is our hope that our report may help to awaken the interest of the public in the history of an ancient American people, as few modern Americans realize the stupendous role the ancient American cultures play in our daily life. Research is bringing this out more clearly every day.

I have not read Frans Blom's journal of the expedition, but one book cites an entry in which Blom wrote that La Farge "is somewhat of a weak sister and seems to hate hard work." However, I did have the opportunity to review La Farge's typed fifty-page journal housed in The Latin American Library at Tulane. In the spring of 2019, Susie and I traveled to New Orleans to briefly inhabit some of the places associated with La Farge's life in that city. One of those places is, of course, Tulane, and I had previously contacted Dr. Hortensia Calvo, Director of The Latin American Library, for permission to peruse La Farge's journal of the expedition. Dr. Calvo and her staff were very helpful during our visit, and she was gracious enough to chat with us about La Farge and Blom, who were intent on "planting the flag for Tulane." She referred me to a short film about Blom titled "Men, Mules, and Machetes," where the explorers can be seen measuring craniums.

I later viewed this nine-minute film, "a picture record from the expeditions of the Middle American Research Institute of the Tulane University of Louisiana" on YouTube, and it is quite the strange documentary. The film is grainy and jumpy and largely overexposed, and an eerie, almost horror-like soundtrack accompanies the opening credits which announce in bold text "Photography by Webster McBryde, Frans Blom, Dan Leyrer, and Douglas Byers." (Douglas Byers, a friend of La Farge's and a member of the third Harvard Navajo expedition in 1924, also traveled with La Farge on the Tulane expedition to Central America in 1927. This expedition resulted in the book *The Year Bearer's People*; more on this book in a bit.) The film opens with a shot of a map of "middle America," and we then see hands weaving a basket. We next view a convoy of horses and pack mules plodding through the countryside before we are shown what appears to be the ruins of a Mayan temple. We witness various men carting large boxes from the structure, then scenes of digging and the uncovering of skeletal remains. By now the film's background music is funereal, almost like an ancient song of lamentation. The movie concludes with scenes of the archaeologists at work, measuring, sketching, taking notes. Blom is clearly visible in his fedora, smoking a pipe. La Farge is not in this film, as he and Blom only traveled together on that first journey in 1925.

So, back to La Farge's journal of that journey, the first entry of which is headed "Vera Cruz, March 12th, 1925," nearly a month after Blom left Tulane. La Farge's notes, which appear below, are full of precise observations expressed in brief declarative sentences:

Up early and into old clothes at last. Steamer in, but mail had not come ashore. Tulane did not think to send it by hand to Cuyamel. Off by crazy little train. Mounds on the right at 11:15 A. M. Palm houses and colour. Guard on train, two small and shabby, but efficient looking soldiers. Open rolling plains and scrub, pot bush. All new and more than interesting. Train rolls like a ship. Lunch at Tierra Blanca, a metropolis—about 75 houses, wood, dobe, and brick. Population accurate. Tile roofs pretty, outlying thatched huts. Hired small boy to watch stuff while we ate; while he watched o.k., but moved our seat. El Hule Cuyamel Banana plantation, large river, mostly flats with flat boats loading bananas, and freight train full. Wood and tin company houses and thatched peon houses. Saw two Tehuantepec women. Bought a bunch of 14 bananas for 10 centavos. Mound group two minutes beyond station, five mounds forming a court. 5:15 open country across a big river with small ? burial mounds, many of them. 6:40 aigrettes in a flock against the sunset. Blue and shadow effects. Flowers grow on trees. 6:55 Spoonbill and Prairie Fire. 7:10 Abreast of fire is distant. El Burro 7:15, Chinese restaurant in hotel, better than I hoped. Bought a comb and soap, as we could not get our baggage. A helpful german called E. Pickenbrok. Trouble getting to bed with mosquitos.

La Farge's stream-of-consciousness observations definitely have a "paternalistic" quality to them, and I am interested in his comments on the banana plantation, as this era represented the zenith of the banana exporting business. In a 1915 essay, "Conquest of the Tropics," Frederick U. Adams, official historian of the United Fruit Company, writes "It is in Guatemala that one begins to appreciate the great civilizing influence of the United Fruit Company." He notes that the Company pays laborers a dollar a day; "what a boon this is to poor Indians." Adams also reports that the United Fruit Company extends financial aid to archaeologists working in the region, but I could find no evidence that the Tulane expedition was thusly financed. However, in the epilogue of *Tribes and Temples*, the authors do thank the United Fruit Company for "furnish[ing] free transportation on [its] lines" and for the hospitality they "received in the camps of [this] company."

One of the reasons Blom was eager for La Farge's participation in the expedition was that he believed La Farge was well-versed on the care of horses and the particularities of camp life. Throughout the trip, the explorers were plagued by problems with horses and mules. Consider this entry from La Farge's journal dated March 23, 1925:

> Off at 9:30 and took the wrong road, losing 1½ hours. So Frans, Henrique, and I took the animals and left the infantry to follow as we could. To Misapa, 4 leagues, to Chacalapa, about 3, and to Chinameca, 2 leagues, all at a trot. Two leagues of straying. The bay pack, laden with arrows and badly packed, distinguished himself by running wild twice and then getting bogged at Chinameca in the middle of the street below the railroad station. God what a brute! I was driving him and a dun at first, but let Henrique take him, and I took the dun who was perfect, and the brown. A bat bit my horse in the neck again. Nasty sight.

Throughout the expedition, it appears that La Farge suffered from periods of bad health. He describes episodes of fevers and chills, and he was occasionally laid low with gastrointestinal afflictions. Maybe the following is what Blom had in mind when he characterized La Farge as a "weak sister":

April 15th, Villa Hermosa to Nacajuca

Slept late and woke with active dysentery, which together with the stench of the town and the flies, made me yet lower and spoiled my enjoyment at the shops along the colonade [sic] where we went to get spurs, etc. At last we mounted about 4:30 P. M. Frans, Gates, and I, a boy, and a mule. Right away I felt better, and as we got into the country with nice smells, a new man.

One particularly interesting entry from the journal is from "Decoration Day," now known as Memorial Day. Two and a half months into the expedition, La Farge seems somewhat despondent as he matter of factly describes the ongoing work, the "constant ethnography" and taking "out pots from tombs." The entry begins with the Latin phrase "Dulce et decorum est pro patria mori." ("It is sweet and fitting to die for your country.") Later in the entry, La Farge reflects further on the holiday:

Today, decoration day, little to do with this Dane [Blom] here, but put our stinking little pennant at half mast and think a solemn thought or two. One would like to make something of it—Harvard-Tulane-Yankee-New Orleans, I mean. That couldn't always have been done.

Perhaps it is the misplaced patriotism of this sentiment that led Dr. Hortensio Salvo to remark that Blom and La Farge were committed to "planting the flag for Tulane."

The last, undated entry of La Farge's journal is written in Guatemala City and is titled "Guatemala in General." In it, La Farge juxtaposes the native hospitality he experiences at the end of the trip with the reception he and Blom received from the American government official, a reception that tempered La Farge's sense of patriotism:

All Guatemalan officials have laid themselves out for us. Herrera (agriculture) especially. We have seen the town and its surroundings, and the market, and all our goods. Entertained by Quintanilla, Mexican secretary of legation, friend of Frans', with American wife.

Very good man. Saw the famous relief map.

But the U.S. Consul has proved to be an entirely improper person, rude, ill-mannered, ignorant, corrupt, and does not attend his duties. It was most unpleasant for me to have Frans see this after the courtesy of all these "greasers." And it has strongly affected my feelings over seeing the flag in far places.

Here endeth the first lesson.

Throughout his public life, La Farge would battle indolent and incompetent government employees, and his disdain for them would figure prominently in his works of fiction.

The expedition returned to New Orleans late in the summer of 1925. It had been a valuable trip for La Farge, providing him with additional experience as a scientist and a writer. He also further developed the habits of mind that allowed him to observe the customs, beliefs, and ways of living of the peoples he visited. As was noted earlier, La Farge resumed his graduate studies at Harvard that fall, but Blom sought and received approval from Tulane President Albert Bledsoe Dinwiddie to hire La Farge as a full time member of the Department of Middle American Research. La Farge moved to New Orleans in early 1926 and immediately took up residence in the French Quarter, "a sort of Creole version of the Left Bank," according to writer Hamilton Basso. Thirty years later, La Farge would describe the neighborhood as "a decaying monument and a slum as rich as jambalaya or gumbo." In relocating to New Orleans, La Farge was living out advice he had once received from his mother. As he writes in *Raw Material*,

My mother told me that in her opinion, every young man should leave his native section for a year or two and go live and work in a strange place where he was unknown. In a way she was thinking along the lines of the anthropological theory that, by the study of alien cultures to which we come with fresh perceptions, we shall eventually acquire a new point of view which will enable us to analyze and understand our own. I found this true in New Orleans, for the culture there was strikingly different from my own, the people and their ways, like the countryside and the architecture, were far stranger to me than England had been.

La Farge was introduced to the artistic community of the French Quarter by Blom and by Natalie Scott, a wealthy acquaintance of the La Farge family with substantial real estate holdings in the city. She owned a Creole cottage on St. Peter Street, where La Farge lived with writer Sam Gilmore. They dubbed their residence "The Wigwam"; La Farge described it as "a place in which we could laugh and sing without causing parents to protest or scandalizing the neighbours."

Soon La Farge was in the process of re-inventing himself. In *Raw Material* he describes his first encounter of a group of young people on a Mardi Gras float:

> I was discovering the glory of a fresh start. The gang on the truck were delightful, *and they liked me.* On my merits only, coming out of nowhere as if dropped by the stork, they liked me. Harvard was nothing to them, Groton they had not heard of ... Something fell away which I had been dragging behind me since I was twelve years old ... I felt deliriously light, I seemed to be someone I had never been. Nobody knew me. *Nobody knew anything about me.* They liked me, God had given me a chance to go ahead and prove myself.

La Farge immersed himself in the creative community of the French Quarter, a community he found invigorating, and soon he was turning out an impressive number of short stories. La Farge later calculated that the literary community of New Orleans probably numbered no more than fifty, and that most of these writers did their best work before or after leaving the city. The latter scenario certainly applies to William Faulkner, who rented an apartment on Pirate's Alley with William Spratling, an artist who taught at Tulane's architecture school. La Farge shared a cook ("a slatternly washerwoman named Lenore who ... cooked food fit for a king") and dining expenses with Faulkner and Spratling, and he was a willing participant in their alcohol-fueled shenanigans. La Farge became known for "his tabletop mock-Indian Eagle Dance," and though he was apparently inexperienced in matters of sex, he soon made up for lost time and developed a reputation as a ladies man. "A bottle of absinthe, some sandwiches, some Saratoga chips were all we needed for a gathering which would last from nine-o' clock to three the next morning," he later wrote. Of course, Faulkner's appetite for alcohol is legendary, but he discovered a willing accomplice in La Farge, and the two created quite a spectacle one night carousing through the streets of town loudly singing the X-rated sea chantey "Christopher Columbo." (In his 1920 biography, *The Life of William Faulkner*, Carl Rollyson convincingly argues that La Farge was the inspiration for Canadian Shreve McCaslin, Quentin Compson's Harvard roommate in Faulkner's *Absalom! Absalom!*)

La Farge's life in the French Quarter, and the lives of his contemporaries there, would figure prominently in his later novel, *The Copper Pot*, which largely reflects Bohemian life in New Orleans, a life "largely conducted at open windows, on the balconies, and on doorsteps, and thence flow[ing] into the street."

William Faulkner, too, would later appropriate his New Orleans experiences into fiction; his second novel, *Mosquitoes* (1927), is a thinly-veiled account of a 1925 boating party on Lake Pontchartrain that included, besides himself, Frans Blom, Sherwood Anderson, and others. As Faulkner biographer Frederick R. Karl writes, "*Mosquitoes* was a jumping-off place ... [and] every aspect of [the novel] radiates out from Faulkner himself: his difficulties with women; his dislike of parasitic pretenders; his ridicule (in Fairchild) of Sherwood Anderson's sentimental views of life; his own sense of the artist as conveyed by the sculptor Gordon; the recurring gender ambiguities; the curiosity about outsiders and even criminals."

In the novel, Dawson Fairchild—Faulkner's fictional stand in for Sherwood Anderson—is depicted as "resembling a benevolent walrus too recently out of bed to have made toilet." And in an oddly prescient moment, Fairchild, in talking about his past, relates, "I got a job helping to fire the college power plant. I could take my books along and study while the steam was up." According to the apocryphal story, Faulkner wrote *As I Lay Dying*, published in 1930, on the back of an overturned wheelbarrow while he was employed to stoke the coal fires of the University of Mississippi power plant. Faulkner even pokes fun at himself in *Mosquitoes* as evidenced by this exchange between two characters, Jenny and "the niece":

> "I got to talking to a funny man. A little kind of black man—"
>
> "A nigger?"
>
> "No. He was a white man, except he was awful sunburned and kind of shabby dressed ... He said he was a liar by profession, and he made good money at it ... I think he was crazy. Not dangerous: just crazy." ...
>
> "What was his name? Did he tell you?" she asked suddenly ...
>
> "Oh, yes: I remember—Faulkner, that was it."
>
> "Faulkner?" the niece pondered in turn. "Never heard of him," she said at last, with finality.

Mosquitoes is replete with vivid descriptions of the French Quarter of the era, as in the following: "Outside the window New Orleans, the Vieux Carré, brooded in a faintly tarnished languor like an ageing yet still beautiful courtesan in a smoke-filled room, avid yet weary too of ardent ways." And, of course, the novel features many words that would become staples in Faulkner's Yoknapawtapha novels, words like "sibilant" and "fecund."

As we have already seen, Faulkner initially came to New Orleans to ingratiate himself to Sherwood Anderson, whose wife Faulkner knew. Anderson championed Faulkner's work and brought the manuscript of *Soldier's Pay* to the attention of his publisher, Horace Liveright, who put out the novel in 1925. During this time, Faulkner was also penning a number of short sketches on citizens of the Quarter for the Sunday magazine of New Orleans's daily newspaper, *The Times-Picayune*. These sixteen pieces, which appeared from February to September 1925, included many motifs and archetypes that would appear in Faulkner's later fiction.

In 1926, Faulkner and Spratling determined to publish a little book as "a sort of private joke" featuring sketches by Spratling of their circle of friends and of themselves. Faulkner would provide the captions of these sketches as well as an introduction to the book. *Sherwood Anderson and Other Famous*

Creoles: A Gallery of Contemporary New Orleans was meant to be a playful tribute to Anderson and his wife, the center of the French quarter social life. However, Anderson was not pleased by his caricature. (Nor was he later happy about his depiction as novelist Dawson Fairchild in *Mosquitoes*. Anderson did not speak to Faulkner for several years after this novel's publication.)

Sherwood Anderson and Other Famous Creoles appeared under the auspices of the "Pelican Bookshop Press" in homage to the literary crowd who liked to hang out at the Pelican Bookshop on Royal Street. The book was printed in a limited edition of 250, "the first fifty decorated by hand with water color and autographed, at $5.00, the others at $2.00." The forty-three "Famous Creoles" pictured in the book were neither famous (with the possible exception of Anderson) nor Creole. Rather, it was a loosely-connected social group linked by institutions such as *The Times-Picayune* and the Newcomb College Art School at Tulane. Easily half of the "Famous Creoles" were associated with Tulane, including Frans Blom and Oliver La Farge.

Faulkner's foreword to the book is decidedly tongue-in-cheek. He begins by describing the Vieux Carré where "forty people … spend day after day painting pictures in a single area comprised in six city blocks." He fictitiously recalls the day that Spratling "came to see me" but "I [Faulkner] did not remember him. Perhaps I had passed him in the street." In this account, Spratling lays his portfolio out before Faulkner, and a bargain is struck when Faulkner agrees to be Spratling's "wheelhorse." This two-page introduction concludes with a brief sermonette on our "universal" American trait: humor. The "trouble with us American artists," Faulkner writes, "is that we take our art and ourselves too seriously." It's clear that *Sherwood Anderson and Other Famous Creoles* is meant to challenge this tendency.

Spratling's caricatures of the "Famous Creoles" are simultaneously whimsical and hyperbolic. His sketch of Frans Blom, captioned "The Tulane Champollion" (Champollion was a French scholar who deciphered Egyptian hieroglyphs), shows the anthropologist lurking on his knees above a thatched hut; he is lifting the roof off the hut as a buxom, bare-chested, and decidedly black "native" flees from the premises. The cartoon is politically incorrect to say the least, and today, if not in 1926, is downright stereotypical and offensive. Which brings us to a little aside on the "Famous Creoles" and matters of race.

Most of the group, of course, were Southerners and expressed the standard white Southern views of the time. La Farge did not necessarily share these views, but he was circumspect when it came to expressing his attitude. If the subject of race came up, La Farge took care not to "flaunt [my] opinions" or "my anthropological theories in the faces of my new friends" and remained reticent. (Or, he lacked conviction.)

Faulkner's caption for La Farge's caricature reads, "Oliver La Farge of Harvard, a kind of school near Boston," which succinctly mimics La Farge's own claim upon first meeting "the gang on the truck" that "Harvard was nothing to them." Spratling's drawing of La Farge shows him in an exaggerated state of repose, lounging with a book in hand, smoking his omnipresent pipe, with a cocktail on the floor beside him.

Susie and I were able to view an edition of *Sherwood Anderson and Other Famous Creoles* during our trip to New Orleans in April 2019. An added benefit of this journey was that we managed to spend a lot of time with our nephew Cortlandt, who has lived in the city for several years. Prior to our arrival, Cort connected me with his friend and soccer teammate Eric Seifort of the Historic New Orleans Collection. Eric met Susie and me at the beautiful HNOC Research Center on Chartres Street, and he and his staff kindly retrieved for us Faulkner and Spratling's book as well other materials tangentially related to La Farge. This was my first trip to New Orleans and I reveled in the sights, music, and, of course, food of this polyglot city. We benefited from Cort's local knowledge and his friendships with young chefs. We made obligatory stops for gumbo, beignets, and poor boys, and trekked one afternoon to Willie Mae's for an artery-clogging meal of fried chicken, collards, and mac and cheese. We had breakfast at Molly's Rise and Shine, the latest venture from Charlottesville native Mason Hereford, whose New Orleans sandwich shop, Turkey and the Wolf, was selected as Bon Appetit's Best New Restaurant of 2017. We dined out at Peche and Pizza Delmonica, and we discovered Fatma's Cozy Corner, a great Mediterranean neighborhood eatery in Tremé. And like William Spratling, Frans Blom, and Oliver La Farge, we commuted between Canal Street and Tulane on the St. Charles Streetcar.

By the advent of 1927, La Farge was firmly ensconced at Tulane, and his picture appears alongside Blom's above a description of The Department of

Middle American Research in that year's *Jambalaya*, Tulane's yearbook. Part mission statement, part advertisement, the description reads as follows:

The Department of Middle American Research, youngest of Tulane's activities, was founded in March, 1924 for studies in Mexico and Central America. While its program eventually embraces the formation of a center of information on all phases of the subjects, in 1925 anthropological and agronomical expeditions were sent out. The past year has been devoted to working up reports of this field work, to the organization of the department, and to ordering and completing its extensive library of reference. At present it gives no courses, but offers the university and its visitors, through exhibits and books, the means of becoming acquainted with the most picturesque and interesting part of the two Americas. Scientists and business men from various parts of the United States and from foreign countries have already begun to avail themselves of these facilities. The department's present plans involve a slow expansion of its field of interest, more exploration, and continuation of its policy of welcoming and assisting visitors. Students of the university are particularly welcome at all times.

However, La Farge was doing much more than attending to the duties of the department; in January of 1927 *Dial* magazine published his Navajo-themed short story "North is Black." The story is narrated by North Wanderer, a Navajo youth who goes on a quest to woo an American woman who had once befriended him. In a moment of reverie, he recalls taking this woman to the top of Blue Rock Mesa, and he tells us that she "was not like most Americans, the way they act. They talk fast, and shout, and spit over the edge. She was quiet, and looked, and thought about it, like an Indian." North Wanderer eventually finds the woman, now engaged. He still hopes to win her love and bring her to his home, and when he discovers her fiancé cheating at cards, he stabs the offender in his hand. North Wanderer is sent away because he has caused the woman's white friends to lose face. Returning home alone, North Wanderer agrees with his mother when she says he needs a wife. Despondent, he tells her, "You will ask for one," and he tells us, "But I did not care if she were old or young, beautiful or ugly."

This story, which was later included in Edward J. O'Brien's anthology *Best American Short Stories for 1927*, deals with many motifs that permeate La Farge's subsequent fiction. Questions of identity, assimilation, and the problem of alcohol are explored in this story and, as we will see, in the novels *Laughing Boy* and *The Enemy Gods*. Furthermore, these themes suffuse much of the contemporary writing by and about Native Americans that we will examine in this book's afterword.

In her 1999 essay, "Anthropology Discovers the Maya," Carol A. Smith details the methods of two basic schools of anthropological research in use in Guatemala in the 19th and 20th centuries. One school, which had its roots at the University of Chicago, "chose small, nucleated settlements where a particular problem focus" could be selected. These anthropologists tended to concentrate on a specific topic like the economy or the life cycle of the tribe in question. The second school of thought originated at Columbia University with Frans Boas, who taught his students to seek out traditional communities in remote areas, communities exposed to minimal modern intrusions. These scholars should mine the essence of Mayan life and "rely heavily on key informants for information about beliefs and traditions." Clearly this second modus operandi was adopted by Oliver La Farge and his friend Douglas Byers when they departed New Orleans for Guatemala in February 1927. This two-man expedition ultimately resulted in the 1931 publication of *The Year Bearer's People*, "mainly the work of one writer"—that writer being La Farge.

The book contains a preface of sorts in the form of a letter from Frans Blom to Tulane President Albert Bledsoe Dinwiddie. In the letter, Blom explains the scope and mission of the expedition:

> Few people realize the task before these two men. Their objective was to investigate the ancient and secretive religious ceremonial of a tribe of Indians which had been persecuted by well-meaning missionaries for about 400 years. They were to conquer the suspicion

of the Indians and gain their confidence. Their task can be likened to that of a man trying to become familiar with the ritual of a masonic lodge without becoming a Mason himself. Outwardly there was nothing spectacular about their work. They would have to spend long and monotonous days wandering around among the natives in hopes of finding a clue to some secret ritual.

The first chapter of *The Year Bearer's People* is essentially a primer on the history of the Mayan people and their conquest. Then La Farge recalls how at the end of the 1925 expedition the local Indians in the village of Jacaltenango were amazed when the anthropologists inquired about the Year Bearer, one of the four spirits in the Mayan calendar that name a year. Thus, the purpose of the current expedition, La Farge writes, is to investigate "the survival of old beliefs and customs that may help us in understanding the ancient culture," a culture inextricably linked to the Mayan calendar and the Year Bearer. In undertaking this investigation, La Farge and Byers hope also "to present the ethnology of the Jacalteca Indians *per se*."

The book goes on to relate how La Farge and Byers went about their business once they had settled in Jacaltenango. They knew that some of the Indians "possessed important secret information" and that they, the anthropologists, would have to "ingratiate" themselves to get at this information. Their plan simply was to be friendly and do their best to learn the language. Eventually this plan was abandoned when La Farge and Byers fortuitously met Senor Don José Maria Hernandez C, "such an informant as one might dream about." Don José Maria was a man with some knowledge of the wider world who spoke a bit of English yet was intimate with the Jacalteca and "acquainted with the finest shades of the language." As La Farge writes, Don José Maria was "the man to whom we undoubtedly owe what success we obtained."

So, what was this success? Certainly, La Farge and Byers gained an understanding of the Mayan calendar and its role as a guide to life, although its primacy in Mayan ceremony and ritual had clearly diminished over time. Additionally, the scholars were able to compile a "grammar" of linguistic material of various dialects. In *Raw Material*, La Farge reflects upon the nature of research, writing "the only way to do … research is to roll in it, become soaked in it, live it, breathe it, have your system so thoroughly permeated with it that at the half glimpse of a fugitive possibility everything you have learned so far and everything you have been holding in suspension is in order and ready to prove or disprove the point." La Farge had clearly been "soaked" in research while in Guatemala, and when he and Byers returned to New Orleans in the early summer, he was on his way to becoming an accomplished Mayan scholar.

However, La Farge was soon vacillating between two paths. In June of 1927, he met with a member of the editorial staff of the Houghton Mifflin Company. This editor had read "North Is Black" in *Dial*, and he asked La Farge about writing a book-length story on a similar theme. In truth, La Farge was already engaged in such an enterprise. He wrote his brother Christopher a letter in July 1927 stating,

> I've started a novel. It is a most painful process, for here, in this weather, a long day at the office really exhausts one. I've been dabbing at it since last November and have now written eighty-five sheets, or about 20,000 words. I have about twice as much to go, and the comforting realization that everything I have done will have to be rewritten.

As he continued to work on the novel, La Farge weighed the wisdom of possibly abandoning a promising career as a linguist and ethnographer, a career he enjoyed and for which he was clearly suited. In September of 1928, Tulane made his decision for him. While at Harvard doing research for Tulane, La Farge inquired about a paycheck he had not yet received. Tulane responded that he had been fired the previous month (without notification) at the instigation of a trustee, whose children La Farge had insulted during an alcoholic rage at a masked ball in 1926. He was given seventy-five dollars in compensation from President Dinwiddie. La Farge returned to the French Quarter to finish *Laughing Boy*, the novel that would both launch and secure his reputation as a writer.

Hermione Lee, in her biography *Willa Cather: Double Lives*, proposes that "Dramatic early dislocations often make a writer." This seems to be true for Oliver La Farge. Removed from his New England upbringing and the blue-blood trajectory and acquaintances of his youth, La Farge was free in New Orleans to pen a story of Indians in the American Southwest.

As he once observed, "It was while crossing Euterpe Street in New Orleans that suddenly the general scheme of *Laughing Boy* took form." Despite this "Ah ha" moment, the idea of the novel had been in his mind for years; he had struggled, however, with how to shape it. He debated how best to bring the story to life, to translate all he knew about the Navajo in a manner that would do them honor but also make their way of life understandable to outsiders. Progress with the novel was slow; when he began the book he was still writing short fiction and working to draft reports for his full time job at Tulane. When he lost his job, he was, in a sense, unburdened and could focus on his fictional account of the Navajo. In *Raw Material*, La Farge reflects on the relationship of his material to his frame of mind at the time:

> *Laughing Boy* expressed the point which I had reached. I saw our own Indians as inexorably doomed, I saw that they must come increasingly into contact with our so-called civilization, and that (I then thought inevitably) contact meant conflict and disaster. I put this idea into the book, along with anger at certain evil things I had seen, and then I let myself out by sending my hero, after the final tragedy, back into my own dreamland, the untouched, undisturbed Navajo country where the white man was not a factor and would not become one in my time. The whole treatment was specific, personal to the characters involved. It might prove good publicity, but it could lead to no reforms.

La Farge goes on to write in his memoir that he was "soaked in Indian literature" when he began to compose *Laughing Boy*. He comments that as he went along in the story he was surprised to note that all of his sentences were short. He worried about this stylistic idiosyncrasy, but acknowledged he was incapable of writing any other way, and was comforted by the work of Hemingway, who executed a similar technique. (Not only did both authors employ short sentences, but both also relied on "short" words. A study of the language employed in *Laughing Boy* reveals that 73.8 percent of the text is monosyllabic. The same study shows that Hemingway's *A Farewell to Arms*, also published in 1929, is 78.2 percent monosyllabic.) Commenting further on the writing of *Laughing Boy*, La Farge states that he was compelled to complete the story because he might never again see the "blessed country" of the Navajo, and, therefore, "in this book I should pour out all my love."

He writes in the 1929 "Introductory Note" to the novel that

> I have been as accurate as possible about ceremonies, rites, and customs. If occasionally I have taken liberties, I plead a writer's privilege. Any innovations I may have made are more the less true to the general pattern of Navajo ideas.
>
> This story is meant neither to instruct nor to prove a point, but to amuse. It is not propaganda, nor an indictment of anything. The hostility with which certain of the characters in it view Americans and the American system is theirs, arriving from the plot, and not the author's. The picture is frankly one-sided. It is also entirely possible.

I find this introduction strangely curious in that La Farge seems to be distancing himself a bit from the narrative, a narrative that, as we have observed, he later proclaimed reflects "anger at certain evil things I had seen."

In 1962, a year before La Farge's death, Houghton Mifflin reissued *Laughing Boy*, "the first authentic novel of the Navajo Indians," with a new foreword by the author who refers to himself in the third-person. He writes: "This book was written about a people who have now vanished, by a young man, now long gone, whom once I knew intimately." He goes on to say that today

> [The Navajo] are an unhappy people, sullen towards all others, unfriendly, harassed by drunkenness, their leaders at once arrogant

and touchy. Still, here and there among them you can still find the beauty, the religion, the sense of fun, you can still attend a ceremony at which no one is drunk. In the space of thirty years, however, the wholeness has gone, the people described in *Laughing Boy*, complete to itself, is gone.

Despite this pessimistic assessment, La Farge is comforted by the fact that people still read *Laughing Boy*, a notion that "would have completely staggered that beginning writer." That writer could not expect in his "days of aching hope and profound self-doubt" such sustained interest in the novel. Therefore, La Farge poignantly concludes, "That leaves the gratification to me, his successor, who am much older and much more in need of encouragement."

Laughing Boy is a linear story, beginning in 1915, that spans eighteen months. The novel is framed by two ceremonies: the book opens at a warm-weather religious festival, the Navajo Mountain Chant, and ends with the Night Chant, which is held in late fall/early winter. During this time, the two protagonists—Laughing Boy and Slim Girl—meet and fall in love with tragic consequences, as Slim Girl tries to navigate the demands of two disparate, yet merging cultures.

The novel begins with Laughing Boy, a silversmith, en route to the Mountain Chant ceremony, as "his insides all were *hozoji*," (2) in harmony with the gods. That harmony is immediately tested when he first encounters Slim Girl, who "had on more silver, coral, turquoise, and white shell than he had ever seen on any one person." (8) He is simultaneously attracted to her beauty and her skills as a dancer, but he is puzzled by her initial behavior, which he finds insulting. Soon, however, he is totally smitten by this "butterfly," this "hummingbird," (29) and despite Slim Girl's caution not to, Laughing Boy determines that he is "going to speak" (32) to Wounded Face, his eldest uncle, the next day. This conference does not go well. His uncle warns,

> "She is a school girl." The tone was final. "She was taken away to that place for six years."
> "That is all right. I like her."
> "That is not all right. I do not know how she came to be allowed to

dance. They made her stop. Water Singer let her dance, but we stopped
him. She is bad. She lives down by the railroad. She is not of the People
any more, she is American. She does bad things for the Americans ... I
tell you, she is all bad; for two bits she will do the worst thing."

Laughing Boy sat up suddenly. "You should not have said that,
you should not have thought it. Now you have said too much. I hope
that bad thing follows you around always. Now you said too much.
Ugh! This place is too small for me." (38)

After this encounter, Laughing Boy goes off to "wrestle with the gods,"
(57) while Slim Girl, who "did not intend to love anyone," (57) but who sees
Laughing Boy as the "light with which to see her way back to her people ...
turned to loneliness as a tried friend and counselor." (58)

However, Laughing Boy and Slim Girl commit themselves to one another
when they next meet, and she kisses him. Laughing Boy "did not understand
it ... Vaguely he remembered that Americans did this ... [and] he had a
feeling of messiness and disgust." (92) Still, "hunger was dead where she was.
She was not like the People; life with her would have to be different, but the
trail was beautiful." (95) Slim Girl also introduces Laughing Boy to drinking,
yet another American habit he does not understand. She uses alcohol as a
"hobble around [his] feet so that [he] will not go away from me." (112)

The couple enjoys a period of true blissfulness where life "was solved
and perfected," (113) and "Laughing Boy went like a swift, quiet river under
cottonwood trees." (113) However, Slim Girl continues to deceive Laughing
Boy with her paid relationship with her American lover, George Hartshorn,
who is increasingly jealous of her time away from him. Laughing Boy admits
that there are things about her that are beyond him, and he notes that when
she returns from her work in town, she is often tired, "and once or twice he
had surprised in her eyes a puzzling look, a look of a man who had just killed
and scalped a hated enemy." (129)

Laughing Boy and Slim Girl travel to T'o Tlakai, to visit his people, who
are Slim Girl's enemies, "more than if they were Utes." (142) Her fears seem
justified when Mountain Singer, leader of the Clan, tells Laughing Boy that
"you are just a light from her fire, just something she has made." (171) But

Laughing Boy counters, "I have been with that woman many moons now. I tell you that I know those bad things are not true ... We do only good things. Everything good that I have known, all at once, could not make me as happy as she and her way do." (175)

Laughing Boy and Slim Girl settle again into a life of domesticity, a life of *hozoji* where "the loom-frame hung near the door; on the other side was the anvil," (198) a life where Laughing Boy "was bringing her back into her people." (200) One obstacle to their happiness is Red Man, who Laughing Boy had once defeated in a wrestling match, and who longs for Slim Girl, who is increasingly haunted by her arrangement with George. And despite his own happiness, Laughing Boy recognizes that "I am losing myself. She holds the reins and I am becoming a led horse." (220) His disquietude is echoed by his friend, Jesting Squaw's Son, who says,

> I have lived in your house, I have seen you. You are both happy, I think; you are both in love. But you are afraid. All the time you are enjoying yourselves you are watching for something over your shoulder, I think. I do not understand this. It is what I saw. This life of yours, it all looks like The People's life; only her going into town is strange. But it is not just she, it is you both that are not living like us, I think. I do not know what it is, but you are wearing moccasins that do not fit you. The sooner you both come back to your own people, the better, I think. (242)

Jesting Squaw's Son proves strangely prophetic when Laughing Boy discovers Slim Girl in the arms of George Hartshorn. He tells Slim Girl, "You have killed us both, I think," (248) and he calmly shoots an arrow into her left forearm which she has raised in front of her face in self-defense. As Laughing Boy says to himself, "The arrow only grazed you; it has gone through my bowels," (251) and he debates whether he should stay with Slim Girl or leave her. Slim Girl professes her love for Laughing Boy, who has brought her back to The People. Of her relationship with George, she says, "I thought it right that an American should pay tribute to you and me, I thought it was the perfection of my revenge." (265) Laughing Boy makes peace with himself and

Slim Girl, telling her, "You have deceived me, but you have not been untrue to me, I think." (267)

The couple decides to go the North to live among The People in a place where there are few Americans. On their journey they pass by a canyon where they are observed by Red Man, who believes he has been wronged by Slim Girl and who fears Laughing Boy. From a distance, Red Man fires at the travelers:

> Laughing Boy heard the shots, turned, and ducked as two bullets snapped close to him, before he saw Slim Girl slump forward in the saddle. He threw his arm about her, caught her rein, and drove the horses at a gallop. The pack animal, startled by the rush behind him, raced ahead. When you only have a bow, and an unseen person or persons begins shooting liberally with a rifle, it is no time for gestures of valour or revenge. (276)

Slim Girl, who Americans had "spoiled … for a Navajo life," (278) dies and is buried as a Navajo. The book concludes with Laughing Boy vowing to cherish the memory of Slim Girl: "The remainder of his life would be a monument to her. All this world could not be changed or taken from him." (285) Furthermore, he realizes that he and she would "never be far from each other," and as he rides away to the Night Chant Ceremony, he repeats, "In beauty it is finished, in beauty it is finished, in beauty it is finished." (296)

La Farge submitted the manuscript of *Laughing Boy* to Houghton Mifflin in May 1929. The book was selected by the Literary Guild, and the novel appeared in November. It was an immediate success, ultimately selling 250,000 copies. *Laughing Boy* was awarded the Pulitzer Prize for Fiction in 1930 and within two years of its release, foreign publishing rights had been sold in Holland, Sweden, Germany, Norway, France, and Poland.

So, how do we account for the novel's popular success? According to La Farge biographer D'Arcy McKnickle, in *Laughing Boy* La Farge "brought outlandish subject matter into the realm of acceptable experience." His artistry lay in his ability to give readers a sense of participating in Navajo life by blending Navajo beliefs and customs with imagery familiar to the polite society of the East. Clearly, as another critic writes, "the key to [La Farge's] success as a writer [is] his perception of the alien Navajos' similarity to ourselves." Another strength of the novel is the depiction of Laughing Boy himself. His innocence and trusting personality allows the reader to shed his own restraints and openly embrace the Navajo life and territory. Laughing Boy's naiveté and lack of a frame of reference for the world of the Americans engenders the reader's sympathy.

For me, La Farge's greatest success in the novel is his handling of the character Slim Girl and her search for identity. Slim Girl is more than a female who is defined merely by her physical attributes; rather, she is a character who acts, and as a dancer, her attractiveness is her kinetic beauty. As she goes about her daily tasks, she "turns utilitarian motions into part of a dance." As a "woman of the world," Slim Girl understands the best and the worst traits of the Navajos and the Americans. Her forced years at boarding school have made her bitter, so much so that she tells Laughing Boy, "If ever they come to take a child of ours to school, kill her." (78) As the novel begins, Slim Girl laments that she is not a Navajo; to win Laughing Boy's affection, she learns to weave skillfully, knowing "that being able to make something beautiful is important to him." (113) Indeed, with Laughing Boy's help, Slim Girl ultimately repudiates her "Americanness" and fully embraces Navajo life. This decision strikes a resonant chord in us as readers in that we, too, often wish to cast off the sins of our past and cling to that which will make us anew and, presumably, better.

La Farge's knowledge of and attitude towards Navajo life also imbues the novel with great authenticity. His scientific field work with the Navajo provided him with first-hand knowledge of the tribe's beliefs, customs, and language. When asked about La Farge's success as a writer, one prominent museum official in 1930 replied, "I don't give a damn about his writing. I don't give a damn for literature. I am interested in science, and he is a first-rate anthropologist. We need him. He's the only man who can talk to the Indians and get anything out of them." In *Laughing Boy*, La Farge writes convincingly of Navajo commerce, religion, and family life, among other quotidian concerns. In the commercial realm, we see the Navajo trade for pleasure and not for material gain, and we come to see the paramount importance of religion in everyday life. In fact, the novel is infused with religion, from the tribal ceremonies to the description of Slim Girl's funeral. Indeed, to describe his love for Slim Girl, Laughing Boy must rely on religious imagery:

> I have been down Old Age River in the log, with sheet-lightning and rainbows, and soft rain, and the gods on either side to guide me. The eagles have put lightening snakes and sunbeams and rainbows under me; they have carried me through the hole in the sky. I have been through the little crack in the rocks with Red God and seen the homes of the Butterflies and the Mountain Sheep and the Divine Ones. I have heard the Four Singers on the Four Mountains. I mean that woman. (158)

This sense of authenticity impressed Mary Austin, a Southwestern writer who was on the committee that awarded La Farge the Pulitzer Prize. On *Laughing Boy* she commented, "I do not recall a single other long story of primitive love in which the story complex is so completely kept within its native color and tone."

La Farge also displays a thorough and deft understanding of family dynamics in *Laughing Boy*. As the plot unfolds, the reader learns that in Navajo culture girls are valued more than boys, and that a groom lives with the family of the bride to serve as another "provider" for her immediate kin. Marriage negotiations are initiated by the boy's family through the maternal uncle, which is why Laughing Boy seeks out Wounded Face in the beginning of the novel. We learn also that a married man avoids his mother-in-law out of respect and refuses to speak to or look at her. Of course, many of these values are foreign to the basic assumptions of the white man who, presumably, marries for love and not economic considerations. (Well, most of the time.) As one critic writes, "To the People, human nature is neither good nor evil; both qualities are blended in all persons, and there is little an individual may do to alter their realistic proportions." This understanding allows Laughing Boy to forgive his wife's infidelities, reasoning "You have lived in a terrible world that I do not know. I cannot judge you by my world." (267) Although the basic premises of Navajo life may be different from our own, we can, nonetheless, believe that La Farge accurately portrays them.

The critical reviews of *Laughing Boy* were uniformly positive at the time of its publication. Writing in *Bookman* in January 1930, Clinton Simpson calls the novel "an almost perfect specimen of the sustained and tempered, the lyrical, romantic idyll ... It is filled with love, with nature ... morals and religion ... La Farge ... has written a book about Indians ... that is likely to be called ten or twenty years from now, real literature." The New York *World's* review of December 15, 1929, says the book is "a novel of Indian life which bids fair to take its place among the more sensitive and important pieces of regional literature which have come from the forgotten crevices of these United States of recent years." Two months earlier, Edwin Seaver writing in the New York *Evening Post* observes that La Farge's novel "is one of the most pleasurable that have come from the pen of a young American for some time." Carl Van Doren writes of *Laughing Boy*, "[It] is at every point a work of art." In *Wings, III* (November 1929), Van Doren goes on to say that "Some Americans may be surprised that the culture of the Navajo is a complete and rounded one, with traditions, philosophy, art, compelling customs, established ideas and sentiments. Mr. La Farge has shown that this is the case without once saying as much." Finally, a few years later (October 25, 1937), *Time* magazine reports that "*Laughing Boy* has stood out [among novels and short stories about Southwestern Indians] as the best, marked by accurate observation, sensitive understanding of the complex Indian psychology, a respect for their cultural dignity."

While raising questions about the novel's ultimate place in our national literature, these critics largely laud *Laughing Boy* for its sensitive treatment of Native Americans. However, not all contemporary readers agree with this assessment. One anonymous member review from www.librarything.com begins:

> A comment from the back cover, which had I read before I opened the book, would have made me discard the book immediately: "An Enduring American Classic (ah ha ha ha ha ha), Oliver La Farge's Pulitzer Prize-winning first novel captures the essence of the Southwest in 1915. At a ceremonial dance, the young, earnest silversmith Laughing Boy falls in love with Slim Girl, a beautiful but elusive

American-educated Navajo (this rings so false). As they experience all the joys and uncertainties of first love, the couple must face a changing way of life and its tragic consequences."

The reviewer goes on to declare

I had a major problem with the book beginning on page 4. On page 4 alone there were FOUR (4) assholic, culturally insensitive, insulting stupid comments, which proved beyond a shadow of a doubt, that this man, La Farge, learned absolutely nothing of the realities of Dineh [Navajo] life, but instead made up some type of fantasy about the Dineh people that soothed his ego.

After detailing the "assholic comments," the writer ponders,

At first I couldn't understand how anyone could be such a racist moron, but then I read the back of the book and this is what is written: "Oliver La Farge first traveled to Navajo territory on a Harvard archaeological expedition. *Laughing Boy*, his first novel, was awarded the Pulitzer Prize in 1930 as the book that best presented 'the whole atmosphere of American life'; it was the first novel about native American life to receive their praise." That says it all, a misinformed white man, showing off his arrogant "bourgeois superiority" by writing about a culture he falsely thinks he knows and fails miserably while showing himself to be an uneducated fool.

Finally (finally!!), the reviewer concludes,

I'm not even going to return this book to the booksale, I'm going to tear it up and throw it away.

Well, what are my final thoughts regarding *Laughing Boy*? As I mentioned in the preface, I'm still drawn to the novel, although I acknowledge its flaws. To a modern reader in the age of multiculturalism, the narrative can seem a little insensitive when La Farge grafts an Anglo value system onto Navajo beliefs and customs. And although I generally reject the overall decrying of cultural appropriation that now pervades society, I do understand why some might claim that a white man could not/should not write from a Native American perspective. But isn't doing so a testament to the power of the imagination? And there does seem little dispute that La Farge possessed an exhaustive knowledge of Navajo life and language. Today, my "issue" with the book concerns the manner in which La Farge, as author, inserts himself into the fictional narrative. These intrusions are meant to be informative and explanatory, but I often find them distracting. Consider this example from Chapter IV:

> Navajos almost never say thank you in return for very great favors; ordinary gifts and kindnesses are offered and accepted in silence. They regard our custom as obsequious. (53)

This is an interesting tidbit, and it does offer insight to the context of the narrative in that moment. Still, I wish La Farge had found a way to reveal this custom—or lack of custom—in a more active way.

The same observation could be made of a scene in Chapter XVI when La Farge deviates from describing Laughing Boy's encounter with alcohol:

> Liquor, taken in solitude, sometimes has this effect. Along with a megalomaniac sense of his central position in the universe, a man grows bluntly honest with himself. All the secrets, forgotten, stifled thoughts come out of the closet in his mind, and he must face them in turn, without a saving sense of proportion. This was now Laughing Boy's portion. (218)

Certainly there is truth in La Farge's words, truth born no doubt from his own experience, but the tone of the passage seems a bit "preachy." And as Mark Twain once wrote, "Don't say the old lady screamed. Bring her on and let her scream."

My quibbles aside, I still love *Laughing Boy*, and the story still holds me in suspension, much the way it did when I first read it nearly fifty years ago. The book is honest and unblinking, and it presents an "alien culture" in an authentic and empathetic manner. I am still drawn to Slim Girl, a vastly complex and entirely believable character. Her struggles are visceral and her life is lived in her nerve endings.

What did Oliver La Farge think of *Laughing Boy*? In his memoir *Raw Material*, La Farge concludes:

> No writer can form a solid opinion of his own work. I know only that I am dissatisfied with mine. Least of all can I judge *Laughing Boy*, for it was a product of a young man whom I have ceased to be and at the same time it is loaded with associations as to make it impossible for me to approach it impersonally. I have a certain dislike for it because it has been so popular whereas my other books have done only fairly well.

Throughout his career, La Farge did resent the disproportionate amount of attention paid to *Laughing Boy* in comparison to his other works. We will further discuss these other works, one of which in my opinion, outstrips *Laughing Boy* in terms of its artistry. That being said, few writers ever crafted a more successful first novel, and after its publication, La Farge fled New Orleans, such a source of creativity and productivity, to return to New York and its familiar institutions and associations. However, we have a bit more business to conduct before we, too, depart the Crescent City.

The circle of acquaintances that comprised the "Famous Creoles" did much to enliven the cultural milieu of New Orleans. They created the *Double Dealer* magazine, the Arts and Crafts Club, and perhaps most significantly, they supported Le Petit Theatre du Vieux Carré, which still exists today. Initially conceived in 1916 by a group calling themselves the Drawing Room Players, by 1928 (when Oliver La Farge was putting the finishing touches on *Laughing Boy*), Le Petit Theatre had 3,500 subscribers; a *New York Times* story of that year proclaimed it "the greatest single cultural force in the community."

The 1931–32 "yearbook" of Le Petit Theatre contains an announcement that states, "In late January, Le Petit Theatre Du Vieux Carré will present 'Laughing Boy' by Otis Chatfield-Taylor, based on the novel by Oliver La Farge."

This announcement goes on to declare (in one very long sentence):

> This will be one of the most interesting and important productions
> ever made by a Little Theatre; interesting because of its novel subjects
> and protagonists—the Navajo Indian, his life, art and philosophy, and
> his attitude toward the white man; important because of the fame of
> the novel; because ours will be the world premiere of the play; because
> David Belasco had the play in preparation at the time of his death,
> because it had already been bought—but not made—by Universal
> Pictures Corporation, because Le Petit Theatre's proposed production
> of it has already received national publicity, and because associated
> with the production will be the author of the play, Mr. La Farge;
> and Mr. Franz [sic] Blom, director of the Middle American Research
> Department of Tulane University.

The play ran from January 25 to February 1, 1932, and in the production's
playbill the Theatre acknowledges "its great obligation to Frans Blom … and
to Oliver La Farge, for their invaluable assistance on matters pertaining
to the Navajo Indian." A list of characters is included of course; Laughing
Boy is played by Felicien Lozes, later a lawyer, while Virginia Mae Barnett
portrays Slim Girl. Besides the speaking roles, the cast also includes several
Drummers, Girls, Young Men, and Women, and one Child (played by
James D. Connell II). The music for the play was composed by Harold M.
Levy from Navajo themes collected by Oliver La Farge, and the dancing was
supervised by Olga Peters.

The playbill also notes that the jewelry, blankets, and many other
props—all authenticated by Blom and La Farge—"have been very kindly
lent by Mr. J. L. Ambrose, of the Crownpoint Trading Company, Thoreau,
New Mexico." The "Company is a U.S. Government licensed trader upon the
Navajo Reservation." Furthermore, these items will be offered for sale after the
run of the play "since the market is being flooded by spurious goods—to the
hardship of the real Navajo art workers—and as the Reservation is suffering
greatly from a very unusually severe winter, the Company is anxious to assist
its wards by the sale of as many of these articles as possible."

There are several "Notes" appended at the bottom of the playbill, including the definitions of certain Navajo terms and an explanation of the Act I "Squaw" or "Forfeit" Dance, in which "girls choose their partners and, whenever there is a rest, the man asks what forfeit he must pay; by the length of time taken by the girl to get down to a reasonable figure, he gauges her liking for his company."

Susie and I perused the Petit Theatre yearbook during our visit to the Historic New Orleans Collection, where we were able to also view photographs from the production of "Laughing Boy." These black and white pictures reveal a set comprised of large monolithic rocks, constructed from I know not what, suggesting a boxy canyon. A few cactus trees appear on the periphery of this canyon, and the whole effect is stark and imposing. Other photos depict the interior of the house, presumably the site of Slim Girl's assignations with George Hartshorn. In several photographs, these settings are peopled by the actors, and the clothing by Laughing Boy and other Indians seems slightly askew to me. The long-sleeved shirts and long pants suggest more of a 1960s Haight-Ashbury look, as do the headbands worn by the "braves." The costumes may be totally authentic—especially if La Farge consulted with the production team—but to me the designs appear to be fulfilling some misguided vision of what "real Indians" look like. And even the shots of the actors seem somewhat off. The gestures of Felicien Lozes look exaggerated and posed in these still photographs. As depicted holding a drawn bow with a notched arrow, he is stiff and unusually awkward, and when he raises his hands in supplication over Slim Girl's dead body, he projects a kind of contrived solemnity.

I don't know what La Farge thought of the play and its staging. Perhaps it represented a kind of approbation from his friends in the city that he had recently left. Perhaps, too, he reveled like a returning prodigal son in his reunion with Frans Blom. However, we don't have to speculate on La Farge's reaction to the cinematic adaptation of *Laughing Boy*, which began filming in Arizona in March 1932, two months after the premiere of the play. La Farge, whose mother, you will recall, referred to him as "Indian Man," took a screen test for the leading role, but he was not selected for the part and became a "technical assistant" on the production. Lew Ayres and Johnny Weismuller turned down the role of Laughing Boy before it was offered to Mexican-born actor Ramon

Novarro, one of the top box-office attractions of the era. In the 1920s Novarro had been featured in the silent films *Scaramouche* and *Ben-Hur*. Marketed as a "Latin lover," he starred with Greta Garbo in *Mata Hari*, released the year before he was cast in *Laughing Boy*. (Novarro, who struggled with alcoholism and with accepting his homosexuality, was murdered in his home in 1968 by two brothers he had procured for sexual services.)

Lupe Vélez, also a native of Mexico, was chosen to play Slim Girl. Known for her fiery personality, she was regularly cast as a hot-tempered exotic or ethnic woman. Velez had a number of lovers in Hollywood, including Gary Cooper, whom she fired upon with a pistol after he broke up with her. She wed Johnny Weismuller in 1933, and their ten month marriage was marred by domestic violence and public fights. She enjoyed a successful film career throughout the 1930s and early forties, during which time she was linked to a number of prominent men. On December 13, 1944, she took her own life when she washed down seventy Seconal pills with a glass of brandy. She was four months pregnant at the time of her death.

It seems eerily appropriate that these actors—both of whom tragically died—would end up playing the doomed lovers Laughing Boy and Slim Girl. However, these box-office stars could not salvage the film. La Farge withdrew from the production because of the "mutilation" of his book, and he never went to see a screening of the movie, which was widely panned at the time of its release. I've not been able to locate the film, either physically or on the internet, but there are a couple of clips on YouTube, including the trailer, which is one of the most "over-the-top" three minutes of cinema I have ever seen. Below is my cobbled together transcription of this preview:

Text	Image
1. From the corners of the world	*Minarets, Chinese junks, African warriors*
2. Off the beaten path of civilization	*Canoes on a jungle river*
3. He brought you romance— adventure	*Close up of man wearing pith helmet*
4. The unusual—the daring	

Text	Image
5. From the tropics —	*Polynesian (?) outriggers*
6. "White Shadows in the South Seas"	
7. With the virgin bride of the pagan temple	*Woman peering through dense foliage*
8. From distant Africa —	*Running "natives" with shields and spears*
9. "Trader Horn"	
10. With "The Cruelest Woman Alive"	*Woman swinging at man*
11. From the Impenetrable Jungle	
12. "Tarzan the Ape Man"	*Cue Johnny Weissmuller*
13. With his mate of the forest	*A "scantily clad" Jane*
14. Now ... Col. W. S. Van Dyke	*Same "pith helmet" man, with rifle*
15. The Explorer Director	
16. Takes you to the Painted Desert	*Solitary rider, mesa in background*
17. ... of the great Southwest	*Large contingent of horsemen in distance*
18. He brings you the epic of	*Female on the ground, stretching*
19. Savage Slim Girl	*Female peeks out from under blanket*
20. The Pulitzer Prize Winning Novel	*Shot of cover of* Laughing Boy
21. Up to now believed too daring to film	*Slim Girl & Laughing Boy embracing*
22. The printed page takes life	*Flipping pages to waving horsemen*
23. Souls are laid bare	*Slim Girl & Laughing Boy kissing*

"Hearts seek understanding … sympathy … love"

Cut to: grown Slim Girl outside of school telling matron: "I'm not behind
wire fence anymore."
Cut to: Laughing Boy and companion galloping across landscape.

Cut to: Laughing Boy's puzzled face; Slim Girl saying, "It is called kiss."
Cut to: Slim Girl in house preparing to go out.
Cut to: Slim Girl in town; derisive looks from loafing men.
Cut to: Slim Girl in George's arms; Laughing Boy enters, draws arrow.

"Ramon Novarro is Laughing Boy—Lupe Velez is Slim Girl—The Saga of
a People—Laughing Boy."

The music that accompanies the trailer is dramatic and brash, and it
does much to enhance the bombastic and caricatured nature of the video.
Throughout the clip, the "savage" Slim Girl is stereotypically portrayed as a
manipulative temptress with a shrill, shrewish tone of voice. Laughing Boy, on
the other hand, seems to exist in a perpetual state of wonderment and gullibility.

The other YouTube vignette shows a brief scene of Laughing Boy talking
to his family about Slim Girl. Their voices are flat and stilted, and they sound
like a group of laconic Midwestern farmers discussing whether or not it
might rain by sundown. No wonder La Farge severed ties with the film and
retreated to the canyons of New York. Before we follow him there and leave
New Orleans for good, let's take care of one more bit of business.

Perhaps you are wondering what happens to Frans Blom, La Farge's
erstwhile mentor and colleague. Blom, who was known for wearing the
clothes of a Mexican peasant and who encouraged his friends to call him
"Don Pancho," was a heavy smoker of Turkish cigarettes who enjoyed "several
daily drinks." He married in 1932 and divorced six years later, subsequently
losing his job at Tulane in 1940 because of his alcoholism. He moved to
Mexico where he met and married Swiss photographer Gertrude "Trudi"
Duby. In 1950 the couple bought a large house in San Cristobal de la Casas in
Southern Mexico, which became a scientific and cultural center welcoming
guests from around the world. Blom died at age 70 in 1963, the same year as
Oliver La Farge.

PART III: NEW YORK

A FTER THE SUCCESS OF *LAUGHING BOY*, OLIVER LA FARGE retreated to New York and ensconced himself into that familiar world. In retrospect he regretted this hasty move, for as he writes in *Raw Material*,

> [*Laughing Boy*] was the culmination of years of hard work and stubbornness, it was something entirely mine, spun out of myself, an achievement as unspoiled as my quick friendship with the people on that truck [in New Orleans]. But most unfortunately I hurried from New Orleans back to my little nest in New York, back to where one could still believe that the old securities continued. I sloughed off almost everything New Orleans and trouble had taught me and postponed the enjoyment of life by another decade.

Despite his obvious personal regrets, the decade of the 1930s saw La Farge flourish as a writer and as an advocate for Native American rights. He published three novels between 1931 and 1937, as well as a slew of short stories and important works of nonfiction. He was politically active, first as the president of the Eastern Association on Indian Affairs, and years later, after that organization's dissolution, he assumed the leadership of the Association on American Indian Affairs. Yet despite these outward signs of success—or, perhaps, because of them—La Farge's personal life was a source of frustration and unhappiness.

On September 28, 1929, Oliver La Farge married Wanden E. Mathews, who came from a socially prominent family with an active interest in music, art, and literature. La Farge set himself up as a lecturer and a writer, and soon the young couple had two children: Oliver Albee (later known as Peter), born on April 30, 1931, and Anya Povy, who came along two years later on August 17, 1933. Oliver and Wanden's marriage suffered from the outset from financial problems. The uncertainty of the publishing market weighed heavily on La Farge, and he fretted that the "Indian material" would run dry, as would the public's thirst for such stories. With his mother's approbation, he resisted the temptation to write more commercially accessible books, books which could have helped to relieve his anxiety about money. As his mother wrote Oliver in 1935,

> I am delighted with your writing. Take time out for the moment— don't do potboilers. You need no practice. What you need is leisure time to expand and exchange a conception, to complete and fulfill it, so it is not sketchy. To write another *Laughing Boy*, you must write from a full mind.

His work with Indian advocacy was not financially remunerative, and his sacrifice of time and energy on behalf of this cause further strained his marriage. During this time La Farge also began to question his role in his privileged class, and he began exploring ways to disassociate himself from this social milieu. Memories of Indian camps, "the tricky rhythm tapped out on a drum, a clear voice singing, and the sound of laughter," haunted him, and increasingly he felt the need to be in and of that world. Wanden likely did not fully share Oliver's affection for the land of the Navajo, where she and Oliver had spent their honeymoon, and after six years of marriage, the couple separated; they divorced two years later, Wanden citing Oliver's "cruelty" as grounds for the marriage's dissolution.

Undoubtedly, Oliver's serious drinking problem and his repeated infidelities contributed to the couple's ultimate estrangement. Once, when Wanden was hospitalized, La Farge reputedly moved another woman into their house in her absence. According to Wanden, Oliver bought presents for this other woman using money given to Wanden from her father as a wedding gift. Years later, Wanden and Oliver's daughter Povy described her parents as stubborn and unyielding, and mutually responsible for the dissolution of their marriage. Furthermore, recalled Povy, neither parent was particularly interested in the young children. But the terms of the divorce awarded custody of the children to Wanden, with Oliver retaining minimal visitation privileges.

After the divorce, Oliver's circle of experiences and acquaintances evolved:

> As I detached myself more and more from uptown New York and my centre of social gravity moved toward Greenwich Village and Santa Fe, my contact with people who were also engaged in a constant struggle to pay the rent through the arts in order to be free to practice the arts steadily increased. The feeling that came with it was one of having been long dessicated and put back into water. I was beginning to discover where I belonged.

However, that discovery of belonging took time, time during which La Farge worked tirelessly to raise awareness of the plight of the American Indian. In 1930 he became the director of the Eastern Association on Indian Affairs, a position in which he investigated the policies and actions of the federal government's Bureau of Indian Affairs. As he wrote in *The Changing Indian* (1940), until the end of the 1920s "all Indian policy was predicated upon the concept of a dying culture and a dying race." He reiterated this point the next year in *As Long as the Grass Shall Grow* when he wrote, "All [government officials] were united in the philosophy of de-Indianization ... and all are joined in the next great attack upon the fundamentals of Indian life: land, unity, religion." The facts certainly give credence to La Farge's contentions: Indian tribes possessed 139 million acres (larger than the state of California) when Congress adopted the Allotment Act in 1887; by 1930, Indian land measured only 47 million acres.

So, what is allotment? According to Anton Treuer, "Allotment is the practice of taking tribal land, which was held in trust for the common use of all tribal members, and splitting it into parcels to be owned by each tribal member, with the remaining land sold to settlers and private companies. The profits from the land sales were then to be used by the Department of the Interior to fund assimilation programs for American Indian people." One such "assimilation program" was the boarding school system. In *The Heartbeat of Wounded Knee*, David Treuer writes, "If we look back to the period now, it is impossible not to feel a kind of sickness at the thought that the government stole Indian land in order to fund the theft of Indian children." As another critic of this policy writes, "Six-year-old Navajo children were snatched from their parents and taken to schools sometimes a great distance from their homes. There they were plunged into a way of life so different from anything they had ever known that bewilderment, frustration, and the warping of personalities resulted on every hand." And if the children did not die at school, La Farge wrote in 1931, they "return[ed] as strangers, ill-adjusted, less able to deal with life than the fortunate ones whom the schooling had missed, usually more dishonest, and imbued with a deep hostility toward white men that is alien to the natural Navajo."

Certainly, this "hostility" was evident in *Laughing Boy* when Slim Girl instructed her husband that if they ever had a daughter he should kill her rather than allow her to go to an American school. As we shall soon see, these schools are a primary focus of La Farge's novel, *The Enemy Gods*.

During the 1930s (and beyond), La Farge never hesitated to criticize Indian Affairs' administrators, missionaries, and other "friends" of the Indian people. These friends, La Farge explained, "could not see the beauty of a Tewa Eagle dance, were deaf to the clear music of a Kiowa singer, unable to imagine good in the wild majesty of the Navajo Fire Ceremony." La Farge further notes that white people, in general,

> fail to look on the Indian as a human being, but regard him as a curious sort of phenomenon either admirable or contemptible, but always devoid of the rounded character and complete nature which they ascribe their fellow whites. I think it can be safely said that the average white person in Indian country never actually sees an Indian, but only the projection of his own preconception.

As has been noted, La Farge wrote assiduously during the decade of the Great Depression. He penned 2,000–3,000 words a day and rewrote extensively. In March of 1930, he began work on his second novel, *Sparks Fly Upward*, and the book was published in the fall of 1931. Appearing on the heels of *Laughing Boy*, *Sparks Fly Upward* soon could be found on bestseller lists in major markets across the country. However, the novel was a limited success. Like *Laughing Boy*, *Sparks Fly Upward* was concerned with the fate of Indians; but unlike La Farge's first novel, the Indians in this second effort were found in Latin America, a region of little interest to most general American readers.

The style of the novel is reminiscent of *Laughing Boy*, in that La Farge again relies heavily on the use of monosyllabic language; seventy-three percent of the words that comprise the novel can be thusly characterized. And in my mind, *Sparks Fly Upward* improves upon La Farge's tendency to lecture the reader in his first novel. There are fewer direct intrusions of editorial content, and the action speaks more explicitly for itself.

The plot of *Sparks Fly Upward* draws heavily from La Farge's experiences in and knowledge of Guatemala, and he wrote the novel while he was proofreading his draft of *The Year Bearer's People*. On the back dust jacket of *Sparks Fly Upward*, Oliver La Farge is identified as "the son of Grant La Farge, the architect, and grandson of John La Farge, the painter." Furthermore, we are informed that "La Farge makes his headquarters in New York City and spends his summer holidays in Rhode Island, but with very little provocation sets off for Central America or the Southwest, where the Indians greet him with a ready welcome. He feels more at home in moccasins and flannel shirt than in the most up-to-date Fifth Avenue apparel."

The novel's title comes from Job 5:7, which says, "Yet man is born into trouble, as the sparks fly upward." Esteban is indeed born into trouble, and as the story begins he is an infant secured in a sling worn by his mother, Serafina, as a battle rages around them. Serafina is looking for her husband, a muleteer who has joined the army, but she finds instead the gravely wounded Captain Gerónimo Cerromayor y Ramido. Serafina leads the Captain to safety, and he tells his deliverer, "I shall repay you." (12)

The narrative jumps forward many years to the wedding of the fifty-two year-old Don Gerónimo to seventeen year-old Doña Favia Villansuela y La Rada. Also in the household is the now deceased Serafina's son, Don Esteban de Cerromayor—raised by Don Gerónimo—who is "all Indian, black hair, black eyes, cheekbones, round chin, and the characteristic, square-cut lips." (24) Don Esteban works as a horse trainer for his surrogate father, and he soon falls in love with the beautiful and exotic Doña Favia:

> Day and night, sleeping and walking, working and resting he was obsessed by Doña Favia … He cut out the 'Doña' in his mind, and chanted 'Favia, Favia, Favia.' Of everything he had ever known, she alone was not a creature of Cerromayor, Villansuela, and her beauty, that was like a proclamation, did not depend on anything. He was aware of that, he was confusedly aware of her as a symbol, as he was of the pureness of race in her beauty. Had one opened his mind and spread it forth, one would have had difficulty determining which possessed him, the girl or the archetype. (52)

For her part, Doña Favia is intrigued by Esteban, the apparent antithesis of her husband. As we are told, "This man was young, he was brave, he had temper. There was danger in him, under all that subordination. He rode beautifully. She just wanted to look at the fringe of that interesting danger." (68)

When local Indians mount an insurrection, Don Cerromayor chooses Esteban to lead the forces to suppress the uprising. Esteban does so, despite his twinges of sympathy for the Indians, a people Doña Favia characterizes as "murderous animals." (79) Esteban's success in the skirmish prompts Don Cerromayor to tell his son, "I have come to the conclusion that you are naturally fitted for the military career." (84) The idea pleases Esteban, though he is loath to leave Favia, and he frets about how he, the natural son of the peasant Serafina, will fare among the well-born young men of the military. Before he departs for service, Esteban and Favia embrace and kiss passionately; she tells him, "Go with God—and—come back." (91)

Soon Esteban experiences triumphs in the barracks and in the bedroom, but "these affairs in no way affected his feeling for Favia; that was love, the others were part of a man's normal processes." (94) He transfers to the regiment of his deceased biological father, Esteban Perez, and in doing so, he begins to question his allegiance to Don Gerónimo. He accompanies the regiment to break a siege at Chuulob, and along the way he saves a young Conapena Indian girl, Marta, from rape. She follows him, and he is promoted to Captain after a skirmish with the Indians. In a subsequent battle in the depths of the jungle, Esteban is the only officer to survive. He is given command of the regiment, and with Marta, "he was a man with a home, and peace around the hearth." (171) The regiment ultimately experiences great success, and Esteban returns to the home of Don Gerónimo, where Favia "was there in the candlelight, unchanged, but he who had seen many women of many kinds could realize now how perfect she was." (177) The two renew their clandestine affair, and "there was nothing in the world he feared, nothing he could not master." (184)

Esteban returns to his regiment and to Marta, and after they separate briefly, she tells him, "About the end of the rainy season, we are going to have a child." (216) The regiment is ordered to seize land now occupied by Indians. Despite his misgivings, Esteban knows he must follow orders:

> [He] cursed the Spaniards for ever having come to this country, he cursed the man who taught him how to read and write, he cursed himself for thinking. He cursed ejidos and Indians, coffee fincas and Tierra Caliente. He damned the President, and analyzed Mendoza's generations in an epic whirlwind, he described every last detail of Suarez, his habits and his guts and his perverse amours. Then he smashed a bottle on the floor and damned them all for standing and gawping at him, and falling into a chair, began to fight with dry, groaning sobs. (237)

Esteban's regiment combines forces with the remnants of another, and he is named General. He sets about reorganizing the regiment, and he "ruminates" over the course and purpose of his life, concluding that "the only thing to do [is] to follow his design and find out what he was intended for." (265) He struggles, too, with his relationships with Marta and Favia. "Favia was white velvet, Marta was golden leather, a woman to campaign with you.

He saw the two in two separate compartments of his life, wondering how long he could keep them separated." (255)

Esteban renounces the patronage of Don Gerónimo and gradually realizes that he (Esteban) "was a child of the Revolution," (278) an acknowledgment made more real when Marta bears a son, "his son, the line continuing ... not Indian, not Ladino, but this new thing, Altureño." (285) However, Esteban still yearns for Favia:

> Ay Dios, what a tangle! He was a man between two knives; whichever way he turned he wounded himself. How could he choose between these things, as though he had to decide which eye to cut out? This child at least was clear, and something to cling to. A red-brown little devil, by God, with plenty of lung power, his son. That was definite. (285)

When a state of emergency is declared in the Republic of Altureño and revolution seems imminent, Esteban is made Minister of War in the provincial government in Olintlan. Don Gerónimo is killed in the battle that follows, and Esteban concludes that "the Indians had torn the line between himself and Favia." (307) The army liberates the capital after a fierce battle, and Esteban essentially saves the country. His new headquarters is the destroyed Casa Cerromayor where "he saw Favia as he had never seen her before, as a person, just a woman; sometime, without his consciousness, he had ceased to need the sureness and height she symbolized ... [and] he simply thought of a woman, and he didn't care." (320) The book concludes with Esteban's understanding that "all the lines were coming together ... in himself and Marta, and he would be at peace now." (322)

I enjoyed *Sparks Fly Upward* for its well-drawn scenes of war, and of course, for the depiction of the doomed love affair between Esteban and Favia. But the most compelling component of the book is Esteban's search for self-identity. His struggle is palpable as he tries to reconcile his humble biological background with his aristocratic upbringing. His ultimate determination to forge his own path is somewhat reminiscent of Slim Girl's repudiation of American influences in her quest to become a true Navajo. However, I am not surprised that La Farge experienced limited critical and popular success with *Sparks Fly Upward*. Without a thorough grounding in Guatemala's colonial history, it is difficult for the reader (or at least this reader) to fully appreciate the class, ethnic, and racial divisions that plagued that country. A clearer understanding of the distinctions between the Spanish, the Indians, and the native populations would make the narrative easier to navigate and comprehend.

La Farge made a conscious decision to turn away from the anthropological nature of *Laughing Boy* and *Sparks Fly Upward* in his next novel, *Long Pennant*. Published in 1933, *Long Pennant* takes place during the privateering days of the War of 1812 and is set in locales very familiar to La Farge: the Narragansett Bay of Rhode Island; the coastline of Mexico or, perhaps, Guatemala; and New Orleans. His publisher received the manuscript with enthusiasm, effusively writing La Farge:

> It seems to me without question the best work you have done. It is singularly objective and singularly Inward—objective by reason of your real imaginative grasp of the subject matter and inward through the exceedingly skillful use of the memory flashback ... It ought, it seems to me, greatly solidify your position among the few contemporary American novelists who really count.

And indeed, *Long Pennant* should have been La Farge's greatest success to date. His writing is nuanced and controlled, and his characters, who represent familiar types to La Farge, are finely drawn. However, the book did not sell well; perhaps the material and New England archetypes had more regional than national appeal.

The plot of the story is inventive, and it is told through the eyes of several prominent characters. These characters are largely introduced in Chapter I: "Private Armed Brig *Glimpse*, of Chog's Cove, Rhode Island." In the very opening we learn from Mr. John Disney, Mate, that the vessel has been absent from home for three years:

> In three years things settle, change, are overlaid, renewed. Three years blended of loneliness and numerous people, monotony and

excitement, the irritation of serving as second in command, and under a younger and less godly man, the strange sensations of combat, the pull of avarice against the fear of consequences which he called conscience, whenever, as now, they touched the edge of piracy, the strain of dodging British men-of-war—with or without all this, a three years voyage on a smallish vessel is long, cruelly long. (1)

We discover in this first chapter that the crew of the *Glimpse* has captured what they presume to be a Spanish sloop, and with a storm now imminent, four men are assigned to man the impounded vessel. The chapter ends with Captain Dodge destroying most of the papers of the captured sloop and lamenting to himself, "Piracy, plain piracy—I'll never forgive myself. Spanish crew, all three of them. American vessel. My God." (17)

The action next shifts to the perspective of Samuel Waterman, Able Seaman, one of the four men riding out the hurricane aboard the sloop. One of the crew is soon lost overboard, and the three survivors—Waterman, Roger Hall, and Ephraim Brown—wake up shipwrecked on a beach where they are approached by "two small, brown men clad only in shorts." (31) The sailors are led to a village, and Samuel, in a fevered state, longs for home while Roger and Ephraim, enjoying the palm wine and the "naked savage women" (39) seem less inclined to effect a plan for leaving. Meanwhile, the crew aboard the *Glimpse* learns that the war is over, and the ship heads to New Orleans to refit and get supplies. Each crew member is paid, and one "ordinary seaman," Jeremiah Disney (nephew of the first mate), decides to stay behind as the *Glimpse* prepares to part for home. Disney settles accounts and tells Captain Dodge, "I'm twenty-six, Captain ... I can get good pay as a rigger here, sir, and I want to make my own way." (65)

However, in New Orleans, Jeremiah soon succumbs to the pleasures of the flesh, and his dependence on drink causes him to be sick in spirit and body. Through the eyes of Ezekiel Nyas, Quartermaster, we board the *Glimpse* on the last leg of its journey home. The crewmen are speculating on the value of their lays, their allotted share of the pirated money, and as Nyas reports, "It led to comments here and there, on the question of piracy in taking Spanish vessels. One man opined that the loss of the last prize, with four good men aboard, was a punishment, maybe." (91) The *Glimpse* reaches home, and the men receive a settlement of twenty-five hundred dollars each, which leads Ezekiel to conclude, "Home and rich, and never need to go to sea again." (102)

A year passes and Jonas Dodge, the erstwhile captain, continues to think of the four lost men. He accepts the finality of their fate and sets about dispersing their shares to the survivors. He pays the parents of Samuel Waterman and Ephraim Brown, but in his will Roger Hall has stipulated that half of his allotment go to Hope Langdon, a young woman with whom he was in love. The other half of his settlement is designated for the families of the men of his village killed on the voyage; his father, Sam, is to receive nothing. Hope refuses Roger's bequest because she is engaged to John Disney. Jonas Dodge is haunted by his act of piracy and its "loathsome face." (107) Furthermore, he knows that "he had blundered, and he could endure a blunder no more readily than crime." (108)

The scene shifts next to the beach village that has harbored Roger Hall and Ephraim Brown for four years. (Samuel Waterman has died.) Despite the fact that they live with power and "marvelously built" (132) women, the two sailors, Brown especially, long for home. As Brown says, "It's all right here, but we don't belong here. We're Chog's Cove men." (137) The men build a boat and contrive an escape and set sail in the direction of New Orleans, where they run into Jeremiah Disney. Disney informs them that the ship the crew of the *Glimpse* had looted was in fact an American vessel and, furthermore, he has the ship's manifest to prove it. Jeremiah wants money from Hall and Brown, who have sold goods purloined from the village, and he threatens to reveal the crime if he is not paid. Hall demands to see the document, and when Disney produces it, Hall manages to burn the paper. After several months of dissolute living in New Orleans, Hall and Brown determine to go home, and they sign on with the crew of the *Panther*, which is heading to Jamaica before returning to its home port of Boston.

Jeremiah beats them home to Rhode Island, where he tells John Disney, his uncle, that Roger and Ephraim are still alive. He also tells John that the pirated ship was an American vessel, and that he has the means to prove it. John's wedding to Hope is imminent, and he gives Jeremiah money to buy his silence. John and Hope marry, and she is soon pregnant. Jeremiah, an unsalvageable drunk, demands more money, and John considers killing him:

> How deep am I in, oh, Lord. Maybe he'll die. Or I'll kill him. Better hang than go on like this. I can't think, can't sleep. I see him when he ain't thar. I must get free. Sin on sin; thy sin will find thee out. His own iniquities shall take the wicked himself, and he shall be holden with the cords of his sin. (235)

Jeremiah tells Sam Hall about the piracy, lying when he claims to be in possession of the American ship's manifest. He suggests they blackmail Jonas Dodge, who has now entered politics with an eye towards national office. When Ezekial Nyas runs into the intoxicated Jeremiah Disney, he asks him, "What happened to ye? New Orleans do this?" Disney replies, "The money all went, and I sold my soul, only today he's mad and won't give me none. Lend me some money, for God's sake." (265)

When Dodge is visited by Sam Hall, the latter threatens the state assemblyman with blackmail. Dodge concludes, however, that "once you pay blackmail there's no end to it," (272) and he contemplates murdering Hall: "Murder. The circle of error runs through piracy and ends in murder. It won't do. No. He laid his pistol on his desk and sat down, chin in his hands, staring at it. It won't do. But this has to be stopped." (283)

The book ends with the arrival of Roger and Ephraim in Chog's Cove. They visit Jonas Dodge, where Hall learns that Hope has refused his money and is now married (with a child) to John Disney. Ephraim calls on Susannah Benton, his former girlfriend and he soon recognizes, "This is where a man belongs, settled right here with a wife. Buy a Block Island boat and fish, or go into the coastwise trade, and raise crops and have chickens. Lots of fun in foreign places, but this is whar a man lives." (295) Roger, "the angel of the wrath of God," confronts his father and Jeremy, and they fight; he tells Sam that the supposed manifest no longer exists. Roger plans on wintering in Chog's Cove before heading out to "the western plains … and beyond them … thar's the Shining Mountains … likely full o' gold, also Injuns and beavers … Sound[s] like a roomy country." (305)

For me, *Long Pennant* is distinguished by its narrative technique. The multiple perspectives, the cyclical storytelling, the varied plot threads, and the use of flashbacks constitute a stylistic departure from both *Laughing Boy* and *Sparks Fly Upward*. The characters of *Long Pennant* are deeply flawed, and thus, deeply human. They are haunted by their past transgressions, and their subsequent actions are heavily influenced by their troubled consciences. The descriptions of life at sea (and especially the hurricane) are tautly presented, as is life in coastal Chog's Cove. The interlude in New Orleans seems overly sordid, but the perverse lives there of Jeremiah Disney, Roger Hall, and Ephraim Brown represent convincing cautionary tales. La Farge's writing in *Long Pennant* is highly detailed, and the book is deserving of more recognition than it received upon publication.

⁂

Oliver wasn't the only La Farge who was writing in the 1930s. In 1934 Christopher La Farge, Oliver's older brother, published his first book, *Hoxsie Sells His Acres*, a "verse novel" set in coastal Rhode Island. The text tells the story of Walter Hoxsie, a long-time resident of this southern New England coastline, who is contemplating selling 200 acres of his property to developers from Providence. Hoxsie is opposed in his efforts by the "summer people" who have homes in the vicinity, as well as by the native denizens of the neighborhood. It is La Farge's depiction of these various characters that gives the book its flavor.

As mentioned, the novel is executed in verse, Consider, for example, our introduction to Walter Hoxsie:

> These pastures were not always overgrown:
> Once they were plowed and planted; thus it was
> When Walter Hoxsie entered on his life.
> The small, dim antechamber of his youth,
> Through which he struggled in reluctant growth,
> Was peopled with the tillers of the soil.
> Now at the end of his restricted days,

> When weary thought pursued the backward path,
> He was a master of the tempo that
> Informed those older lives; for all of that
> He had forgot the only tune which gave
> That tempo reason.
> Fifty years in days
> Which made their course each by the urgent sun
> Unvarying, regular, counting night as nought
> But the cessation of activity,
> Land to all life the virtue of their beat.

Upon its publication, *Hoxsie Sells His Acres* garnered two reviews in *The New York Times*. The first, by John Chamberlain, appeared on June 15, 1934, and it was followed two days later with an assessment by Percy Hutchinson. Both critics make note of La Farge's "talented family," and both, of course, comment on the author's inventive use of verse, a style reminiscent of Edwin Arlington Robinson and Robinson Jeffers. Chamberlain calls La Farge's verse "a flexible instrument," ranging from hexameters to blank verse to rhyming couplets. This variety of meter allows La Farge to shift perspectives as he explores the minds of the novel's disparate characters. However, Chamberlain concludes that "Mr. La Farge's verse is not always distinguished."

In his review, Percy Hutchinson writes that La Farge's verse-forms are not always appropriate for the mood they intend to convey, citing, for example, La Farge's "unlucky liking ... for a species of hexameter, never a native English meter." For Hutchinson, the success of *Hoxsie Sells His Acres* relies on its "tang," its portrayal of the people and scenery of the Rhode Island shore. The reviewer concludes that the book is both extraordinarily experimental and solidly substantive, and that Christopher La Farge has created a work "that is ingrainedly American, accurate, discriminating, and moving."

As we have already discussed, Christopher La Farge, like his younger brother Oliver, attended St. Bernard's, Groton, and Harvard. His career at Harvard was interrupted by World War I, where he served in France as a Second Lieutenant in the U.S. Calvary. After the war, he completed his education at Harvard, where, like Oliver, he was on the staff of the *Advocate*, the college literary magazine. Christopher went on to study architecture at the University of Pennsylvania, and from 1924 to 1931 he practiced with McKim, Mead, and White in New York City. During that time he also exhibited his watercolor paintings in New York galleries. Christopher joined his father's firm in 1931, but when the Great Depression forced Grant La Farge to close his business, Christopher moved with his wife and two sons to Kent, England, and there he wrote *Hoxsie Sells His Acres*. Christopher and his family returned to the United States in 1934; he split time between New York and Rhode Island, and he contributed stories and poems to the leading magazines of the era. When he died of a stroke in 1956 at age 58, Christopher had published nine books, two of which were main selections of the Book-of-the-Month Club.

Christopher always staunchly supported Oliver's career, and upon Christopher's death Oliver wrote his eldest nephew that Christopher had always been "the kindly big brother toward my writing." The letter goes on to say that as writers at Harvard "he and I assumed that he would get there first and most," but after the success of *Laughing Boy*, "[Christopher] proceeded to take the position that I was the experienced writer and he the beginner."

⤹⤸

In his next novel, *The Enemy Gods*, Oliver again returned to his "Indian material" to write his most overtly political work of fiction. A kind of antithesis to *Laughing Boy*, *The Enemy Gods*, published in 1937, tackles the then present-day realities of the Navajo. La Farge called the novel "a counterpoint to *Laughing Boy*, a real study of what his [Laughing Boy's proverbial] son would be up against today." And as the novel makes clear, that "son would be up against" the racism of government officials and missionaries, all of whom seem determined to strip the Indian of his native identity. As La Farge biographer D'Arcy McNickle writes in *Indian Man: A Life of Oliver La Farge*, "The novel catalogs all the vicious practices, the inhumanities, the stupidities, the outright thievery that had thrived in Indian affairs through three administrations, and what he [La Farge] described were not generalizations but conditions he had himself witnessed or had gleaned from official reports."

Chief among the "inhumanities" that comprise the novel is the system of Indian boarding schools, designed to "kill the Indian but save the man." One of the early firsthand accounts of an Indian boarding school is Francis La Flesche's *The Middle Years: Indian Schoolboys of the Omaha Tribe*, originally published in 1900. The book takes place in the mid-1860s at a mission school founded in 1848 in Nebraska to serve the Omaha tribe. In his preface, La Flesche writes, "It is not my purpose to give a continued story with a hero in the following pages, but, in a series of sketches, to present the companions of my own young days to the children of the race that has come possessed of the land of my fathers." Before presenting these sketches, La Flesche provides the reader with a view of the particularities and practices of the school he attended. For example, regarding the tribal tongue, La Flesche reveals that "When we entered the Mission School ... we encountered a rule that prohibited the use of our language, which rule was rigidly enforced with a hickory rod, so that the new-comer, however socially inclined, was obliged to go about like a little dummy until he had learned to express himself in English."

To further "assimilate" the students, La Flesche notes, "All the Indian boys in our school were given English names, because the Indian names were difficult for the teachers to pronounce. Besides, the aboriginal names were considered by the missionaries as heathenish, and therefore should be obliterated."

The loss of language, La Flesche argues, lies at the heart of white people's "misconception of Indian life and character," and that the absence of identity perpetuates ignorance and prejudice in the attitudes and habits of whites. Furthermore La Flesche asserts, "no native American can ever cease to regret that the utterances of his father have been constantly belittled when put into English, and their thoughts have frequently been travestied and their native dignity obscured."

Thirty-plus years after his experiences at the boarding school, La Flesche concludes the preface by lamenting that

> The white people speak of the country at this period as "a wilderness," as though it was an empty tract without human interest or history. To us Indians it was clearly defined then as it is today. We knew the boundaries of tribal lands, those of our friends and those of

our foes; we were familiar with every stream, the contour of every hill, and each particular feature of the landscape had its tradition. It was our home, the scene of our history, and we loved it as our country.

Writer and anthropologist (and Ojibwe Indian) David Treuer provides a succinct and damning history of Indian boarding schools in his masterful *The Heartbeat of Wounded Knee: Native America from 1890 to the Present*. In his treatment of the boarding school system, Treuer focuses on perhaps the most well-known of such institutions, the Carlisle Indian Industrial School in Carlisle, Pennsylvania. (This is the school where legendary athlete Jim Thorpe played football for coach Pop Warner.) The school was founded in 1879 by Richard Henry Pratt, a veteran of the Civil War, who later served as a second lieutenant in the campaign against the Plains Indians in the 1870s. At Carlisle, as was the case at the mission school that La Flesche attended, students were not allowed to speak their native language and, upon arrival, the boys had their long hair shorn, a tribal ritual often associated with mourning. Punishments were severe at Carlisle and included using lye soap to wash out the mouth of anyone speaking in their native tongue. Daily beatings were often administered, and offenders could also be jailed in an old guardhouse and provided with limited rations. This inhumane treatment is perhaps best illuminated by the graveyard at Carlisle, where hundreds of Indians are buried. Treuer refers to the 1928 Meriam Report, a comprehensive assessment of Indian life, that notes "Indian children were six times more likely to die in childhood while at boarding school than the rest of the children in America." Treuer concludes that the effects of the schools—which separated thousands and thousands of children from their families, their culture, and their religion—are still felt today.

La Farge also wrote about the Carlisle Indian School, in 1956 in *A Pictorial History of the American Indian*. In this book, he calls Carlisle's purpose one of "inspired and brutal benevolence," where "the idea was to break [high-school-aged Indians] completely away from their families and their tribes, forbid any speaking of their native languages or any manifestation of their native culture, and put them through a course of sports that would make them over into white men."

Chapter One of *The Enemy Gods* begins when six-year-old (or so his age is declared to be) Ashin Tso-n Bige first encounters the enrolling clerk at Tsaili Boarding School. The clerk records the boy's last name as Begay, and the first grade teacher, Miss Sparks, says, "Call him Myron. It kinda suits him." (7) (According to author Douglas Preston, "'Begay' comes from the Navajo *Biye'* meaning 'His Son.' Navajos traditionally do not give their ceremonial names or even their common names to strangers, so when young boys were sent to BIA boarding schools and asked their names, they would often reply, 'George Begay,' meaning 'George His Son,' usually as a way of avoiding speaking their real name.")

Myron Begay, as he is now known, has been sent to school by his stepfather. Myron's father died when Myron was three, and his mother and her new husband had two small children of their own. Myron "knew he was unloved," (10) and his stepfather, who believed Myron to be lazy, thought it best to "let Washington feed and clothe him." (10) After his dehumanizing and capricious naming, Myron's disorienting introduction to school continues. His hair is cut and "he knew from the stories his father told at night that one could hardly be a Navajo without it [hair]; it was a sign of the essence, a declaration." (10)

Months pass and Myron, who is very bright, becomes a favorite of one of the religious teachers, Mr. Butler, and his wife. Butler asks Myron if he wants to go home for the summer or stay at the school. Myron accepts the latter option:

> Myron Begay turned and walked slowly back to the others. He would not have to go home and work for that man [his stepfather]. School was hard, but his stepfather was worse than the Disciplinarian. Mr. Bucla [Butler] liked him, really liked him. Mr. Bucla and Miss Winters are nice. Mr. Bucla owns the Jesus trail. He saw the long-haired, blond Jesus, a white *yei* who liked little boys whose fathers had died; like his uncle, only a *yei*, a holy one. Mrs. Bucla gives him cookies. Who wants to be a Navajo? (20)

When Myron's best friend Jack Tease asks him why he is not going home, Myron declares, "I'm going on the Jesus Trail. I'm going to be just like a white man." (39) Later that summer the school hosts a family visiting day for the students who have remained behind. Myron's family does not come, but the father of his friend Homer tells him:

> I think you are making a mistake, too. If you learn all the white man's ways and forget the Navajo, if that happens to our young men, then we die, we are destroyed, as surely as if by warfare. The man who will serve his people in the years to come, the man who will strengthen them, is the man who can learn all of the one without losing the other. That is what we are hoping for, we who used to be warriors and leaders, and who still wear the old-fashioned clothes. (46)

Myron resists this advice as he continues to grow and learn, now at a new school where he excels in the classroom and on the football field. His religious instruction is thorough, and he repudiates his native identity when he declares, "I ain't Navajo, I'm civilized." (64) Now sixteen, Myron is sent home for the summer, and is confused by the languid rhythms of Navajo life, a life that contrasts sharply with the strict schedule of school. He is initially disdainful of his tribal contemporaries, but he soon acquiesces to their way of life. However, after taking part in an initiation ceremony, his sense of cultural displacement is enhanced. He tells his girlfriend, Juniper, that he is "mixed up" and that he has to "know what I am." (181) When he figures this out, he tells her, he will come to see her. She cautions him not to take too long because she might not wait for him, but Myron counters with, "I'm worth something, too. I'm worth waiting for a while." (181)

Myron then trains for ministry at a new school in Santa Fe. He falls in love with a young woman, Ethel, and his rival for her affections is his old friend Jack. One night in town, Myron is attacked by two drunk Mexicans who derisively call him an "Eendian son of a beetch." (253) One of the men slashes at Myron with a knife, and in the ensuing fight the man is killed. Myron retreats deep into Navajo country, feeling "neither Indian nor white, neither Christian nor Navajo, nothing at all, a cypher, a zero." (257) He is taken in by

Ashkaantsoni clansmen and his spiritual dislocation continues: "though he could neither pray nor sing, he thought constantly about God and the gods, going round and round a series of old paths that became smooth and hateful, and restored pain each time at the same points." (267)

Myron probes physically and spiritually deeper into Navajo country, and in his encounters with others he engages in debate about the duplicitous policies of "Washington." He reunites with Jack, who has married Ethel, and it occurs to him that he had never really known Ethel. He visits a settlement of hogahns, where he encounters Juniper. She has married an Indian named Singing Gambler and given birth to a child, but has recently told him not to "unsaddle," a declaration of divorce. In time, Myron tells her that he is Navajo again and wants to live with her; Juniper rejects him and "the days and nights stretched ahead without purpose or flavour, grey and interminable." Myron leaves, but is soon guided to a group of three hogahns where a healing ceremony is taking place for a girl who has "fallen into a twitching sickness." (304) Myron takes part in the ceremony, and the familiar rituals eventually comfort him and restore his sense of purpose. He returns to Juniper more sure of himself and his way forward. He tells her:

> Our world is changed … Just following the old Navajo way won't save us, and we can't walk in the white man's trail. We have to give up a lot of little ideas, that we have held because they were the best we knew. If we want to save ourselves, we have to learn to use the white man's knowledge, his weapons, his machines—and—still be Navajos. (323)

Myron again asks Juniper to marry him when she is ready, because, he says, "just thinking of you when I'm alone makes my blood sing." (324) She promises to consider his proposal and assures him (he is going to see his uncle) that he will be welcome to return to her.

> He did not move or speak. He saw her face against the white rain of the loom, the colours of her dress, the green tree splashed with the yellow sun, and the bright sky behind, and he remembered the smiling faces of the gods. (325)

Thus ends the novel, a story than spans over twenty years from the mid-1910s to the era of the New Deal. It is a realistic story of the Navajo as they become entangled with disingenuous politicians and inefficient government agencies. And while in the summary above I haven't explored the machinations of congressmen and Indian Office administrators, the economic exploitation of the Navajo is a prominent theme in the novel. *The Enemy Gods*, like *Laughing Boy*, dissects the nature of identity, as Myron vacillates between a familiar ancestral path and a new way forward. *The Enemy Gods* differs from *Laughing Boy* in that Myron rejects his "Indianness" at an early age before its vestigial mystical associations connect him with his people. Also, in *The Enemy Gods* it is the hero rather than the heroine who chooses to flee from the white man's society.

The Enemy Gods is a comprehensive look at the Navajo, but Myron's romantic conundrum is sublimated to more political and thus, perhaps, less interesting problems. As a result, *The Enemy Gods* lacks the popular appeal of *Laughing Boy*. Still, I find it an intensely engaging narrative that clearly expresses La Farge's belief that Navajo assimilation into mainstream life need not require the sacrifice of tribal culture and customs.

In addition to the three novels La Farge penned during the decade of the 1930s, he also wrote numerous short stories. His story "Haunted Ground" won the O. Henry Prize for the best short story of 1931, and in 1935 *All the Young Men*, a collection largely comprised of Indian tales, was published. Regarding his Indian stories, one critic writes of La Farge that "he placed a high value on readability, even embellishing or rearranging non-fiction materials to enhance their appeal to readers. At the same time, the scientist in La Farge demanded that portrayals of culture and character be true to his data."

Some of the stories in the volume can trace their roots to *Laughing Boy*. This is particularly evident in "Higher Education," in which the character Lucille is highly reminiscent of Slim Girl. Told by a white man, the story is an unapologetic condemnation of Indian boarding schools and their deleterious effects. The character Joe comments on these schools when he tells Professor (the narrator) of Lucille's return to Navajo country: "Just out of school. Six years in California learnin' to stick her little finger out when she drinks tea, and then turned out to graze in the howlin' desert. Hell of a system if you ask me." And when Professor first sees Lucille, he notes her obvious sense of dislocation:

> The face was Indian; not only the breadth of cheek-bone, fine long eyes and beautiful chiselling of a wide mouth, but the emptiness now drawn over it, the mask of absence which all Indians possess for protection in times of stress and which the school-children above all learn to use. She wore it now. One could not tell what looked through her eyes when she left school, but from then till now, on the train, re-entering the forgotten wasteland of her home, seeing the first of her own ragged people, meeting race-conscious Government employees, shunted about, disregarded, with the almost terror of her old way of life before her, she had put on the mask. She had been learning.

Lucille's father, Wind Singer, complains to Professor that his daughter has forgotten their language. "While we want our children to learn English," he says, "we don't want them to forget the things that have made the Navajo strong." Lucille, he concludes, "is all shame and fear. At night, when she thinks we are asleep, she cries."

For her part, Lucille wants "nice pretty things like white girls have." She is repulsed by the dirty bodies, dirty clothes, and dirty habits of her people, and she laments, "What can I do here?" Soon, however, she takes up with the white trader McClellan, and despite warnings that "he's a bad man," she is attracted to him and thinks he looks like Ramon Novarro. (Perhaps not a compliment from La Farge; as you will recall, Novarro played the title role in the bastardized film version of *Laughing Boy*.) At the climax of the story, Strong Hand and Professor discover Lucille—Running Girl—in McClellan's apartment wearing a "very frilly, elaborate, negligee, pink in colour, and highheeled slippers with big, feathery tufts on them." Strong Hand wants to kill McClellan, but Professor refuses to give him his rifle for that purpose. Later, when Lucille learns that she is pregnant, she jumps off a cliff to her death.

The title story of the collection, *All the Young Men*, reflects La Farge's pessimism about the contact between the red and white races. The story focuses on Old Singer, a medicine man who realizes that "As a man full of needs and wants, I am finished." Old Singer is contemptuous of whites and their intrusions on the society of the Navajo. He is taken in by his granddaughter and her husband Wesley, a bootlegger. Wesley persuades Old Singer to try liquor, convincing him that it will intensify his religious rituals. Wesley builds up Old Singer's habit of drinking until the proud Navajo is totally addicted. Old Singer loses status and self respect and eventually draws apart from his family. He decides to leave the "bad country" and sets off for where Navajos are still men. On his journey,

> Always he saw short hair and the stupid smart expressions of the young men. They wore clothes over clothes. No one stood up clean and straight in breech clout [breechcloth] and moccasins; no one let the sun strike on strong chest and shoulders; no one wore the dignity of the old, strong blankets ... The Navajos were dead; these were the children of the dead people.

Drunk and despondent, Old Singer ends up in a white man's jail, and as he dies, the mystical deity "Slayer of the Enemy Gods ... placed Old Singer behind the saddle on his turquoise horse, wheeled on the rainbow, and galloped up after the warriors, beyond the reaching of white men."

Of this story, La Farge told his brother Christopher:

> It was a cry from the soul, as far as I was concerned, a statement of my feeling of the tragic loss of beauty in Indian life, thoroughly romantic and sentimental, which rises up occasionally all the more violently because it is an attitude which I must sternly repress in dealing with the grim realities of Indian affairs.

The stories collected in *All the Young Men* are powerful, yet understated, and their direct subtlety contrasts with the proselytizing tendencies of La Farge's novels. The compressed beauty of the short story form requires La Farge to succinctly unfold the narrative and refrain from interrupting the plot.

On October 14, 1939, Oliver married Consuela Otille Baca of New Mexico, and the couple moved into an apartment in Greenwich Village, an initial step in permanently separating himself from the society of his family and peers. This separation became manifest the next year when Oliver and Consuela moved to Santa Fe, where Oliver would live for the remainder of his life.

PART IV: NEW MEXICO

OLIVER LA FARGE AND CONSUELO OTILLE BACA FIRST MET Labor Day weekend in 1936 at the annual Fiesta in Santa Fe, and they intermittently corresponded over the next year while Oliver taught creative writing at Columbia University. In the fall of 1937, the couple again rendezvoused at Fiesta; they discovered they shared similar interests and complementary temperaments, and in early 1938 Consuelo arrived in New York where Oliver resumed his courtship of her. She returned to New Mexico in June and later that summer Consuelo and Oliver traveled together to the Hopi country. When Consuelo next came East, Oliver took her to Saunderstown to meet his family, and in October of 1939, Oliver and Consuelo wed in a small private ceremony in New York City. Oliver observed that Consuelo "wore a smart going-away dress and black pumps, which she had selected for herself." While pleased for Consuelo, the Baca family, who were practicing Catholics, were distressed that Consuelo was marrying a divorced man. As a result of this union, Consuelo would no longer be able to receive the sacraments in the Catholic church.

In the early 1950s, La Farge wrote an elegiac account of the Baca family called *Behind the Mountains*. A series of vignettes—most of which were originally published in *The New Yorker*—La Farge confesses that "a book of this kind involves the writer in the dangerous, sometimes deadly business of 'arrangement' [for the] better illustration of a point." La Farge goes on to write in the Foreword that "one of the aims of this book is to record a fairer picture of a way of life that has ceased to exist," a way of life La Farge discovered by "simply sitting and listening to my wife and my in-laws remembering together."

The Baca family lived in Rociada, which "broadly speaking ... covers two villages, the embracing ranch, and the valley in which they lie. The valley is high, long, and irregular, walled by the higher mountains of the Sangre de Christo range, east of Santa Fe and the Pecos, north of Las Vegas, away from everywhere, innocent of paved roads." In the book's first chapter, La Farge writes that "looking back across an abyss of change, my wife thinks of the village of Rociada first in terms of the weddings." A description of one such wedding focuses on the bride's shoes:

> The slippers had been bought not to fit a foot of flesh and bone but to fit an idea. A bride is young, beautiful, Spanish, and her foot is tiny. The dainty, costly slippers would never be worn again. They were for that day, and it was necessary not that they fit Aurelia but that she should conform to them. Consuelo wondered if fathers-in-law liked to make brides cry. In her experience, the bride always did.

The clear focus of the book is Don José, Consuelo's father and a former lieutenant governor of New Mexico. His imperious presence rules the household and governs the behavior of his family and staff. Consider, for example, Don José's expectations for his oldest son:

> Don José's idea of what his son's education should embrace covered a lot of territory. The boy should have a good general education, with Latin, and a sound grounding in the Catholic faith. He should speak correct English and Spanish, and know some French. He should be familiar with the English classics and enjoy the use of books. He should be able to ride, shoot, rope, train horses, and manage sheep and cattle at least as well as any of the men who would someday work under him, and he should master the many aspects, commercial and agricultural, of running a great ranch.

Along with this knowledge and these arts, he must have the manner of a gentleman, according to both the English and Spanish standards. Don José's ambition for his son was saved from unreasonableness by the fact that he himself had all these accomplishments.

Sadly, as La Farge relates, Don José died suddenly in 1924 when Consuelo was twelve years old. Simultaneous with his death, the market for wool and lambs collapsed, and the Bacas, devoid of their patriarch and their chief source of income, eventually sold their ranch and moved to Santa Fe. La Farge describes this change of fortune with great pathos:

> Don José had seemed to them to dominate the landscape as he did the community. He had been getting ready to run for governor of New Mexico, and the odds favored both his nomination and his election; then suddenly he was sick, and then suddenly he was dead. It was as if a piece had fallen out of the sun. It is significant, I think, that all the talk of the old times I have heard from Doña Marguerita and from others has included little more about Don José's death than that it happened. Talk of the years before is full of him; tales of what happened later are dated as after his passing. It is a dividing point of history, but the event itself is not for reminiscence.

When Consuelo was old enough for a paying job, she found work in a title abstractor's office in Las Vegas. As La Farge writes,

> Love will not always be practical; it demands its own expressions. With her first pay check Consuelo made a down payment on a miniature wristwatch with a delicate silver web of a bracelet, which seemed to her to have been made especially for her mother. It was the first wristwatch that Doña Marguerita had ever had, and it would be hard to say which of them, she or Consuelo, was more delighted. For a moment, the girl would forget the chill wind that blew ever stronger. In any case, she had set her foot on the path that led in time to the office buildings of Manhattan, and hence to my own everlasting good fortune.

Behind the Mountains is a deeply affecting work full of memorable anecdotes. There is the story of the Christmas of the crippling snow in which

Consuelo's parents and older brother Pino conspire to keep the holiday alive for Consuelo and her young sisters. Another story details how these same girls bedevil their tutor, Miss Eufenia. And there are empathetic renderings of La Tulisa, the blind woman who cares for her grandson, and of Canuto, the "Alabama Negro," who is a trusted member of the Baca household and who ultimately owns land in the valley and brings the news of Rociada to the displaced Bacas.

La Farge won a Guggenheim Fellowship in early 1941, and he and Consuelo permanently relocated to New Mexico. They moved first to a small house in Tesuque, on the northern outskirts of Santa Fe, and Oliver settled down to write, excited at the prospect of a new beginning. He hoped, too, to make a fresh start with his estranged children who were now living on a ranch in Colorado with their mother and her second husband, Andy Kane. La Farge wrote in August of 1941, "We have been expecting to have Oliver and Povy here, but it turns out Oliver has been behaving very badly, and that his arithmetic is so bad, that he has to make up two years work this summer or fall back a grade." Therefore, the visit was cancelled and as La Farge acknowledged to his brother Christopher, "it's way past time that Oliver and I spent a lot of time together. He's much too surrounded by women, and I want to try my own hand with him." As we will see, La Farge's relationship—or lack of relationship—with his son Oliver would frustrate them both for years to come.

La Farge and Consuelo soon felt at home in their adopted city. La Farge, of course, had visited Santa Fe several times as a young man, first out of casual curiosity before being "staggered by delightful reality into more visits and then moving in," and he definitely had an affinity for the Americans Indians who inhabited the "harsh … insatiable land" of New Mexico. La Farge first wrote about Santa Fe in a January 1931 article for *World's Work* in which he details a trip he and Wanden made around the Southwest. Of their encounter with the city, La Farge writes "the people aside, the town caused a growing sense of disappointment, partly, perhaps, because we had heard too much about it first." He describes the charms of the Governor's Palace, the Cathedral, the Plaza before lamenting, "Above this screen tower great smokestacks, the most prominent objects in the city, [belching] forth soft-coal smoke into an atmosphere sought by many for its purity." He goes on to comment on further attractions of the city and of its residents before concluding, "Santa Fe has the possibility of being, as it was once, unique and fascinating, and it will succeed, if only it does not try too hard."

But in 1936, La Farge embraced the allure of his future home by writing "Why They Came to Santa Fe":

> Because they heard that between these
> mountains in the well where time lies
> still and yesterday's truth waits in
> naked beauty.
> The firewood smells like incense, adventure
> and ease lie down together, but above all
> leisure and contemplation survive.

Later, when he was known and appreciated in Santa Fe, La Farge wrote of his affection for the town as one which has "warmth and rewards that big city dwellers never dream of." Chief among these rewards is "the habit people have of stopping him in the street to tell him that they have enjoyed his last piece. Strangers will sometimes introduce themselves to do this. It is the kind of thing that makes a writer's life really worth living."

⋘⁀

In 1976, New Mexico writer Tony Hillerman edited *The Spell of New Mexico*, an anthology of essays about his native state. The volume includes a 1952 piece by La Farge, and in the book's introduction, Hillerman reminisces about La Farge and his attraction to New Mexico:

> La Farge, as much as any man I have ever known, was tuned
> to people. His sensitive antennae were always fully extended to the
> fellow humans around him. La Farge treasured New Mexico because
> it offered—probably more than any place in America—a rich variety of

human cultures, religions, and value systems, and because it attracted and held an interesting variety of immigrants. If La Farge appreciated the landscape it was because of its effect on the human spirit. La Farge was, first and always, a humanist in the basic sense of the word.

La Farge's essay on New Mexico was originally published in *Holiday* magazine in 1952, after he had been living in Santa Fe for over a decade. He complains in this piece that tourists to the city don't seem to understand that New Mexico is actually part of the United States. He goes on to describe the many cultures that inhabit the state, and he poignantly writes of the plight of the Navajo who "live in deep poverty in their ash heap of a desert, even vainly presenting to the Great White Stepfather a dreadful bill of broken promises." La Farge concludes his essay by rhetorically asking,

> What is New Mexico, then? How sum it up? It is a vast, harsh, poverty-stricken, varied, and beautiful land, a breeder of artists and warriors. It is the home, by birth or by passionate adoption, of a widely assorted population which has shown itself capable of achieving homogeneity without sacrificing its diversity. It is primitive, undeveloped, overused, new, raw, rich with tradition, old and mellow. It is a land full of the essence of peace, although its history is one of invasions and conflicts. It is in itself, an entity, at times infuriating, at times utterly delightful to its lovers, a land that draws and holds men and women with ties that cannot be explained or submitted to reason.

In 1942, Houghton Mifflin published La Farge's fifth (and last) novel for an adult readership. *The Copper Pot* is a curious work that depicts the life of Tom Hartshorn, a displaced northern artist living and working in bohemian New Orleans, a place of "mystery and promise." Tom is "not just a northerner, but the real article, Rhode Island, descended from abolitionists," (82) and clearly a fictional stand-in for La Farge. As D'Arcy McNickle writes in *Indian*

Man, the plot of *The Copper Pot* "closely parallels the course of La Farge's early life. The details differ and, in any case, are immaterial. He is looking at himself from a later perspective, explaining, in part excusing, but most emphatically condemning the inherited and acquired traits" that engendered the personal decisions that shaped his life. The author's "Note" that prefaces the novel seems almost a parody of the standard "This is a work of fiction" disclaimer. In this "note," La Farge writes,

> The true novelist, as distinguished from the reporter of material in fictionalized form, "creates" his characters by a synthesis of many unrelated impressions and observations reaching through his entire life, cemented together by imagination ... The variations of mankind are not infinite and certain elements recur over and over again, this common stuff of humanity cannot be eliminated from fiction, but in any sincere novel, including this one, where any of those resemblances to real people occur they are accidental and unintentional. (v)

La Farge's insistence that "resemblances ... are accidental" in fact encourages the reader to seek out parallels between the life of the author and that of his fictional doppelgänger. And, as we shall see, these parallels are extensive.

Before looking at the novel, two observations need to be made (at least by me). First, it is ironic—or at least mildly diverting—that La Farge's last novel, which depicts life in the French Quarter, was written in New Mexico; conversely, *Laughing Boy*, the author's first work of full-length fiction, was penned in the heart of New Orleans' Vieux Carré, but chronicles life among the Navajo of New Mexico.

Perhaps separation from the respective locales enhanced La Farge's longing for these settings and, as a result, influenced his artistic treatment of them.

The second observation concerns the name of the protagonist of *The Copper Pot*: Tom Hartshorn. What are we to make of the fact that La Farge christened his alter ego with the same last name as Slim Girl's American lover in *Laughing Boy*? You will recall that in that novel, Slim Girl essentially manipulates George Hartshorn to finance her return to the ways of the Navajo and endear herself to Laughing Boy. When he accidentally learns of Slim Girl's arrangement with Hartshorn, Laughing Boy predictably sets in motion the inevitable demise of his own life with Slim Girl. Hartshorn is not a fully realized character in *Laughing Boy*, but he is the tool that severs the harmony between the native lovers. And while one might, I suppose, suggest that George Hartshorn is merely a victim in a doomed love triangle, there is nothing in La Farge's portrayal of him that sparks sympathy in the reader. However, in *The Copper Pot*, La Farge clearly treats Tom Hartshorn with affection. Maybe this convergence of names is purely coincidental and not worthy of consideration. Nevertheless, it seems odd to me that the hero of *The Copper Pot* shares the moniker of a loathsome character from *Laughing Boy*.

The clear theme of *The Copper Pot* is Tom Hartshorn's tension between living the life of an artist versus adhering to the strictures and expectations of his Rhode Island upbringing. The novel features a colorful cast of characters obviously based on the "famous Creoles" of La Farge's tenure at Tulane. The novel's artists and writers habitually frequent the Pen and Palette, "a combination of gallery, book and supply store, and hang out," (3) an establishment undoubtedly modeled after The Pelican Bookshop. Within this milieu, Hartshorn, like La Farge, is somewhat of a ladies' man, or at least he considers himself as such. Within the first three chapters, the reader is introduced to three young women, each quite different from each other and each a potential romantic partner for Hartshorn. On page three, we meet Frances Warren. She "wasn't so tall," La Farge writes, "about five foot seven, but she stood beautifully, with a high head finely balanced. Her hair was almost black with copper lights in it, and her eyes were a true, deep blue. Color, line, and feature, but there was more than that: her presence had quiet and warmth, she was no usual woman." (3)

In chapter two, Tom confesses, "I want—what I want is a girl of my own, who'll be home when I call and here when I want her. Someone like Jenny [his friend, a sculptor]—grey eyes, a wide mouth, and slender, erect body." (7) However, in chapter three, Tom becomes interested in the enigmatic Rita Tanislav who lives in the building next door to his own, and who "may be a floozie ... may be a hooker, and ... may be a damn nice girl." (26) Yet despite his near obsession with women and the female form, Tom concludes "there is no contentment like good male company. No demands, no effort, but a mutual extension of peace and warmth." (49)

The novel provides many glimpses into the artistic process, as rendered by La Farge through Tom. For example, Tom longs to paint the Tanislav house, and in studying it one day, he notices

> The sunlight still lay along the gallery. He saw what had shone now, a huge, very fine copper pot, a beautiful thing in itself and doubly so from this angle because it was full of empty bottles of various shades ... The scene began to arrange itself, he was calculating, selecting, thinking of colors and beginnings, feeling a familiar, detached excitement in the pit of his stomach. (97)

Tom soon begins work on this painting, and when it is done he realizes that "it had dictated its own course, somehow. He had thought unusually little about technique, it was as if someone better than he, wiser, had inhabited him while he was at work." (132) The canvas is chosen for a show in New York where it receives good critical reviews and where it sells for two hundred dollars. But when Tom's uncle and benefactor suddenly passes away, Tom is faced with the loss of the allowance that sustains him at a time when he is "just getting going." (155) Consequently,

> He fell into a sort of self-pitying lassitude ... and he seemed unable to start anything new, for whenever he thought of a picture he was blocked by the feeling it wouldn't sell. This was commercialism, this was the death of art, he wrestled with it, but still he had no heart for fresh work and he began to doubt the essence of his being as an artist. (163)

To make money, Tom creates advertising posters, and with a friend he churns out etchings of the French Quarter for the tourist trade. Eventually he begins work on another large canvas, of a traffic jam on Royal Street, a work that "might turn out to be really good, at some distant time it might even sell, but that wasn't the point. He didn't care if anyone liked it or not." (197)

Tom also gets a job teaching at the Art Institute where one of his students, Estelle Garney, is "a definitely pretty blonde, rich, beautifully dressed, her educated Southern speech further tempered by an Eastern finishing-school influence." (216) Simultaneous to meeting Estelle, Tom becomes reacquainted with Frances Warren, and in time he comes to believe "that he would marry Frances if he could." (223) When he wins a prestigious prize (and $500) for his painting "Jam in Royal Street," he thinks immediately of calling Frances because "she understood what the picture was all about and just what this would mean to him, and he knew how glad she'd be." (235) However, when Tom gets a $1,000 commission to paint a mural at a new hotel—The Golden Gulf—in Houchitas, Mississippi, he runs into Estelle Garney and her family. Estelle is "southern and rich, but there were touches of familiar things about her; she was a girl you might have met in Newport, a girl you might have danced with sometime in Providence or Boston." (247) As the work on the fresco progresses, Tom sees a lot of Estelle and her parents at their "huge plantation-style house [with] lawns, stables, a private dock on a choice bit of beach." (248) He concludes that Estelle "belonged to that life, that way, from which he had been so long exiled," (253) and he proposes to her. She accepts and soon plans are set in motion, plans that include a life in Greenwich Village underwritten by Estelle's parents.

When Tom returns to New Orleans, he experiences serious misgivings about a future with Estelle, a future where he would live "like a pet dog." (267) He spends more time with Frances and after the Pen and Palette Ball, she spends the night at Tom's place. The next morning, "he kept thinking what a swine he was," (277) and later that day he confesses to Frances that he is engaged. They part, but Tom immediately second guesses himself and realizes, "I'm being taken to New York. Taken." (287) He writes Estelle to call off the engagement and runs to Frances's home only to discover that she has left the city. The novel concludes with Tom musing on the nature of art and holding out hope that he and Frances will be reunited:

> The thing to do now is paint. Long for her, and wait, and paint. In
> a little while I'll know where she is, then I'll go and get my answer, and
> then I'll have heaven and I'll paint, dear God how happily, or the long
> emptiness and thank God for painting. And coming soon in its order is

my answer to what I owe the world for being alive to love and paint in it. And when that's paid and answered, if I'm still alive—paint. (295)

At best, the above is a cursory examination of *The Copper Pot*, which features many sub-plots involving the denizens of the French Quarter. Indeed, for me, one of the chief pleasures of reading the novel involves speculation about which characters are based on La Farge's acquaintances in New Orleans in the 1920s. For example, is Bill Cooper, who cashes a check meant for Tom and goes on a drinking binge with the funds, a fictional treatment of Bill Faulkner, La Farge's erstwhile companion? And, of course, there are the moments where La Farge drops his own past into the plot of the novel. When Tom visits Rita Tanislav's room, he is surprised to discover that she possesses an extensive library which includes a copy of *Laughing Boy*. And as news of World War II in Europe becomes more pronounced, Tom must consider his isolationist politics. As a graduate of St. Peter's School, Tom is not inclined to trust the policies of Franklin Roosevelt who is, after all, a Groton man. Finally, Tom, a Harvard alumnus, self-deprecatingly remarks to yet another romantic partner, "You can always tell a Harvard man, but you can't tell him much." (115)

I guess in some respects *The Copper Pot* is a novel La Farge had to write. It is his only work of fiction that does not feature indigenous people, and it is also a work in which he examines the role of the artist in society, but as such, it is a treatise that is often pedantic and preachy when it debates the tension between art and commerce. But finally, it is a novel in which La Farge exorcizes his own past decisions. Unlike La Farge, Tom does not marry the wealthy girl, and he does not temporarily forsake the pursuit of his art. Finally, Tom does not move back East, unlike La Farge who believed his return to and entanglement in his upper class milieu compromised or retarded his commitment to writing.

⤙⤙⤙

When the United States entered World War II after the Japanese attack on Pearl Harbor, forty-year-old Oliver La Farge applied for service in the Air Force. After much bureaucratic delay, he was commissioned as a captain in

March 1943 and sent to Officers' Training School in Miami Beach. It seems that La Farge, who as a young man always bristled at rules and regulations, embraced the strict regimen of military service. This service afforded him a life contrary to the lonely existence that so characterizes the writing life. The man that Tony Hillerman said was always "tuned to people" found himself working alongside men of diverse backgrounds, relishing the camaraderie generated from living in close quarters with others, and serving a common purpose. La Farge immersed himself in this life, and committed to becoming an expert on aviation and the history of the Air Transport Command. In 1944, now Major La Farge co-wrote a short volume titled *War Below Zero: The Battle for Greenland*. In part, the book details the efforts to rescue the crew of an American bomber that crashed into an icecap on November 9, 1942. This effort is characterized by La Farge in the following words:

> Whenever our men have been stranded or cast away, there have been the same determined, combined operations to save them. They belong to the armies of that half of the world which believes that all men are valuable and even a single human being is important ... it would be regarded more appropriate, one imagines, for the men [of the Axis nations] to have patriotically frozen themselves to death having first arranged their bodies in the form of a chrysanthemum or other appropriate emblem.

La Farge's military experience provided him with enhanced self-confidence and a sense of order in his personal life. As he wrote to his brother Christopher, "I'm coming more and more to think that the two best things which have happened to me since *Laughing Boy* are marrying Consuelo and entering the army."

After the war, Lt. Col. La Farge returned to Santa Fe, where he and Consuelo bought a house at 647 College Street. The couple added a bedroom and a study to the home, and the study essentially served as the office of the Association on American Indian Affairs, which La Farge headed. In his new home, the dwelling where he lived the rest of his life, Lafarge settled down to write and conduct his business.

This new home quickly afforded La Farge the vantage point to examine his past, and in 1945 he published his memoir, *Raw Material*, a "fresh and honest personal narrative." The purpose of the book is to "record the America of one individual and to set down the raw material from which the writer derives the finished product he offers the world." In a review of the book, critic Paul Engle writes:

> Out of this autobiography of a successful writer comes the figure of an honest, intelligent, active, and altogether intense American. It was a curious life he had, a unique life among the millions of men his own age, for it went to preparatory school to Groton to Harvard to the Navajo Indians to New Orleans to Central America to New York and to the Air Force. It was a wide life, and it could, given its origins, so easily not have been. That it pushed beyond the edges of an easy acceptance of the remote life of the Groton boy becoming the Groton man was due solely to La Farge's energetic resolution and his necessity to find his own special way. The book is, in fact, a study of his efforts to beat out of the deep room in which family and custom had placed him, to tear down the barriers between himself and other kinds of people, other classes, other occupations.

I have thus far quoted extensively from *Raw Material* on La Farge's effort to "tear down the barriers" of his past. I've found his essays on his education, his tenure in New Orleans, and his experiences in Navajo country particularly informative and illuminating. However, the book's first chapter—"In the Expectation of War"—is enlightening in that it is essentially a treatise on the art of writing and, as such, it informs all the "raw material" that follows. In the beginning of the essay, La Farge declares, "All writing is in one sense autobiographical." Still he laments the tendency of readers to seek literal connections between a novelist's work and his life. (Guilty!) As an example of this proclivity, La Farge recounts how many female readers of *Laughing Boy* comment to La Farge that his wife surely was the inspiration for Slim Girl. To which, "the only reasonable answer," La Farge writes, is 'Certainly, madam, I got her out of a sporting house.'" La Farge goes on to say that "the artist ... is his own chief source of material," and that "his own experiences and perceptions are in the truest sense his raw material." He continues his reflections on the art of writing in "Main Line," the last chapter of *Raw Material*. Here, he acknowledges that while it is "fatiguing work there is no pleasure comparable to writing ... Making love is equal to it but unfortunately, that does not last long enough." For La Farge, writing is "a life rather than an occupation," especially when composing a novel:

> Everything else will revolve about this for six months or more; you will eat, breathe, and sleep it, think of it at odd times, and find all other interests dominated by the idea of the completed job—and wonder what the completed job will be like. The story changes as it grows, you constantly surprise yourself.

La Farge credits "the Indians" for giving direction to his writing life, for they required that he try "to tell the truth, as far as I could learn it, about actual people [and] that my whole study of Indians had ... a purposefulness which was real in fact." He concludes, "This enabled me to disguise from myself the nature of what I was doing." In other words, La Farge's training as an anthropologist and ethnographer ostensibly planted the seeds that allowed his life as an artist to bloom.

The end of "Main Line" (and thus the end of *Raw Material*) is an affirmation of the artistic process. Much like Tom Hartshorn concluding statement in *The Copper Pot* that he *must* paint, La Farge affirms that

> You write. You spend your life in pursuit of something you will never catch ... the good, the beautiful, and the true. They are all one ... [and] a writer finds ultimate beauty and goodness in ultimate, absolute truth, a brilliance of which the human mind can catch no more than glimpses. It lies in your idea, in your intention. In the story you are about to write you see the gleam of one fragment of universal truth, you see the possibility of that beauty. And you write.

Raw Material is a very personal book, and like its author, it is often enigmatic in nature. In it, La Farge reveals himself as egotistical yet self-effacing; confident, yet insecure. However, as one La Farge biographer notes, *Raw Material* "is written with grace and charm. La Farge eschewed crudity in his writing. The autobiography must rank as one of his best, if not the best, literary efforts." I agree. In *Raw Material*, La Farge casts an unflinching gaze at his life, and in doing so, he examines the forces that shaped him as a scholar and an artist. The writing is indeed graceful and compelling as it recounts the many chapters of La Farge's life, a life in which La Farge forged a unique and resolute version of the man he intended to be.

By the late 1940s, Oliver and Consuelo were firmly enmeshed in their lives in Santa Fe, and in the fall of 1947, Consuelo became pregnant. Oliver, then forty-six years old, was delighted by this news and the prospect of starting a second family, as his encounters with young Oliver and Povy were virtually nonexistent. In early 1948, Consuelo prematurely delivered a baby girl who suffered from a gastric obstruction. Despite surgery, the child survived only a week. Three years later, on December 28, 1951, John Pendaries La Farge was born, and by all accounts the new addition to the family was adored by his fifty-year-old father.

A few months before John's birth, La Farge began writing a weekly column for the Sunday edition of the *Santa Fe New Mexican*, a column he continued to write until two weeks before his death in 1963. This "general commentary on the local scene" generated about 350,000 words during the thirteen-year course of its publication; many of the pieces were posthumously published in 1966 in *The Man with the Calabash Pipe: Some Observations by Oliver La Farge*. In his introduction to this volume, its editor Winfield Townley Scott writes of La Farge, "Whenever I was with him—and I was with him uncounted times for nearly a decade—I felt the deference one should feel to that rare person who keeps the possession of a rich education and a great facility in the employment of it." Scott goes on to call La Farge a "testy" man, one who "held opinions strongly—and if you disagreed he could marshal his facts dismayingly." Furthermore, according to Scott, La Farge "could be a tough *hombre* in his demands on others as on himself, but his skin was thin." However, despite La Farge's irascibility, Scott concludes his introduction with this anecdote:

Thomas Wentworth Higginson, writing from Newport nearly a century ago, said, "I ought not to complain of living in a place which has John La Farge ... He is one of the few men to whom it is delightful to talk—almost the only one with whom I can imagine talking all night." In a far and different town many of us felt just like that about John La Farge's distinguished, unforgettable grandson.

I very much enjoyed reading *The Man with the Calabash Pipe*, especially La Farge's pieces concerned with "The Ways of Words." Many of these columns lament "the degradation of the meaning of words,"—the fact that so many words are incorrectly or obliquely used. He acknowledges that "all my objecting will probably do no good at all, but it helps me blow off steam." I know how he feels. As a middle school English teacher, I too sometimes despair over the current state of our language, in which so many words have lost their piquancy and our written discourse often succumbs to trite and hackneyed phrasing. (Don't get me wrong; I know that I am more than capable of producing the awkward phrase or using a word in a "confuzzled" manner.) Yet despite my despair, there is the delight I discover when one of my students writes a composition that uses language in fresh and arresting ways. For as La Farge writes, "Good English, correct, standard English, sharp and definite in meanings, vast in range, infinitely varied in vocabulary, capable of the most phonic manipulations, is a writer's dream language."

Finally, one column from *The Man with the Calabash Pipe* speaks directly to me and my own personal experience. Writing in the 1950s about education, La Farge states, "Educationists are the bunch that dreamed up and now make important hay out of the idea that, instead of requiring that teachers be learned or thoroughly versed in a subject, they should study something that educationists call 'education.'" Okay, I concede that education schools have their place, and it is certainly important for teachers to be well-acquainted with current pedagogy and best practices. But I consider my own teacher-training to have been a colossal waste of time (and money). When I decided at age thirty to pursue teaching, I enrolled in a state college to get certified to teach high school English in Virginia's public school system. In this college, I learned such valuable skills as how to operate an overhead projector or mimeograph machine. (Remember them?) And for reasons unknown to me, I was required to take a personal health class where I was told it was never wise to eat a large pepperoni pizza and drink a six pack of Budweiser by oneself. Why not, as La Farge suggests, let teachers "be learned and thoroughly versed" in the discipline they teach? For as La Farge goes on to complain, "[Educationists] have gone far towards establishing the rule that in our public schools, a well-trained historian is not competent to teach history, a skilled and enthusiastic mathematician to teach mathematics, unless he has also taken courses in education. Not knowledge, not scholarship, but M.Ed., or preferably Ed.D. degrees are the requisite for tenure and promotion."

So, back to my own experience. After taking the requisite education courses, I still could not be certified to teach English, despite having an undergraduate degree in the field and, at the time being also enrolled in a Masters' degree program in English. So why was I unable to gain certification in English? Because I had no undergraduate classes in math or laboratory science! And why did I have no such classes? Because I was busy taking English classes! Even though the University of Virginia had granted me a B.A. degree in English (and did not require that I take math and/or laboratory science classes), I now found myself enrolled—with a considerable sacrifice of time and money—at the local community college taking biology and some sort of hybrid math for dummies. Upon the successful completion of these classes and passing the requisite state exams, I finally received the Commonwealth's stamp of approval, and I was promptly hired to teach 10th and 11th grade English in Virginia's largest public school jurisdiction. Ten years later, a public school colleague and I started our own school, a school administered by a small group of passionate and autonomous teachers well trained in their disciplines—with not an "educationist" in sight.

La Farge's *Cochise of Arizona* was published in 1953, eleven years after *The Copper Pot*, and because of its limited length and focus was deemed intended for young readers. The story, La Farge writes in the preface, "is fiction based

on fact." The characters are "historical" and "the main incidents are also true."
(5) The novel chronicles the hostilities between the Chiricahua Apaches, a
band of 300 warriors led by Cochise, and the U.S. Army.

In the opening chapter, La Farge describes Cochise as

> well over six feet tall, well made, strong. He was nearly fifty years old,
> but he moved like an athlete. In the Apache style, his long hair fell to
> his shoulders on either side of his face. Around his head a piece of blue
> cloth was bound.
>
> His face was strong and stern. Many who knew him have
> described him as handsome, in an Indian way, with a high nose, wide
> cheek bones, and a firm mouth. (7)

As the story begins, the Chiricahuas are at peace with the White-Eye
soldiers, but this peace is threatened when another tribe, the Pinaleños, kidnap
a Mexican boy, the adopted son of rancher John Ward. Despite evidence to
the contrary, Ward blames the Chiricahuas for Miguel's abduction. Mexican
soldiers seek revenge for this act, and when they kill some Apaches, Cochise
announces, "We must punish so that it will not be forgotten." (43) He leads a
raid against the Mexican garrison in which the Chiricahua capture livestock
and weapons, and kill a score of soldiers.

Initially the U.S. Army takes no action to recover Miguel, but circumstances
change with the arrival of Second Lieutenant George N. Bascom at Fort
Buchanan. Two years removed from West Point, Bascom believed

> all Indians were liars, thieves, cowards, and murderers. He did not quite
> hold that they should all be wiped out. But he was convinced that the
> only argument that they could understand was force, and if necessary,
> brutality. He was sure that it was simply silly to think that any Apache
> chief would keep the peace, no matter what promises he had made. (69)

When Bascom meets with Cochise, he calls the chief a liar, and as a result,
"The white flag had been violated, the peace had been broken." Formal war
ensues. As La Farge writes,

It almost seems as if the two sides were competing to see who could do the worst. White men at the time justified their acts by pointing to the deeds of their enemies. This was not a very good argument for people who proudly stated that they were civilized and Christian, and that the Apaches were ignorant savages. It is not by his enemies but by himself and his own standards that a man of honor judges his acts. (100)

The Chiricahua enjoy success in this conflict despite being heavily outnumbered. Familiar with the terrain, they engage in hit-and-run warfare and routinely evade the "blue-coated cavalry." But with the cessation of the Civil War, more settlers and troops arrive in the Southwest and the tide begins to turn against the Apaches. Cochise continues to lead raids against scattered settlements and, in the eleventh year of the war, he makes fifty-four attacks against the enemy, killing forty-seven "White Eyes."

Eventually, a peace is negotiated. Boundaries are established and the Chiricahuas are allowed to keep their weapons. This peace lasts as long as Cochise and Jeffords, the white negotiator and Indian agent, are alive. As La Farge tells us, "Not until many years later did other white men prove once more that they would not keep their word. With sudden force they drove the peaceful people out of their mountains and moved them, like prisoners, to a dreary, half-desert reservation far from their homes."

I think it fair that the publishers of *Cochise of Arizona* marketed this novel to young adults. The book is full of gripping action, and as such it reminds me of the many works of adventure I read as a boy, works such as *Tarzan* and Robert Louis Stevenson's *Treasure Island* and *Kidnapped*. Illustrated by L. F. Bjorklund, my edition of *Cochise* is full of dramatic pen and ink drawings. The physical dimensions of the volume are also smaller than a standard text, and the larger font size practically guarantees that the book will be a "page turner." And like many works intended for younger audiences, there is no debate as to the hero of the tale. La Farge's sympathies clearly align with Cochise and his followers as, with a couple of exceptions, the white people are portrayed as deceptive, disingenuous, and cruel. La Farge writes, for example, that Lieutenant Bascom feels "the lives of Indians were considered to be of no value. It was believed that the only thing they understood was brutal force, and it was all right to lie to them or to violate a flag of truce." (107)

On the other hand, "Cochise's word was sacred. He never told a lie; he never broke a promise." (18) As Jeffords says of him, Cochise "is a man of honor. He always keeps his word." (172) Furthermore, Jeffords explains that Cochise "is deeply pious. He gives a good deal of his time to prayer and to thinking about his religion." (172) La Farge clearly extols Cochise's virtues, but as he laments in the novel's last sentence, "The bones of the great chief lie in peace in his native land, but possibly somewhere his soul knows that the peace he made was not kept to the end after all." (191)

In 1959, the University of Oklahoma Press published *Santa Fe: The Autobiography of a Southwestern Town* by Oliver La Farge with the assistance of Arthur N. Morgan. As Paul Hogan writes in the foreword, "This book, composed from the columns for the *New Mexican*, is the autobiography of Santa Fe throughout the last hundred years." And as La Farge details in the editor's preface, "The *New Mexican* first appeared in the little town of Santa Fe, capital of the vast, wild territory on New Mexico, on November 28, 1849." La Farge goes on to say that the purpose of the anthology "is to give the feel of the city and, secondarily, the Territory and state as they went changing down the years—an autobiography of a community like none other in the United States, perhaps like none other in the world." Indeed, even a casual perusal of this compilation of one hundred years of columns reinforces Santa Fe's unique social history, a history forged in a melting pot of ethnic and artistic cultures. In fact, from its beginning, the *New Mexican* "consisted of four pages, two in English and two in Spanish."

Much of the commentary in these pages is concerned with matters pertaining to Indians. The November 14, 1863, edition reports that

> The Navajoes are on their walks for plunder: Look out, ranchers, for your herds and flocks. On Thursday of last week, about nine miles below Santa Fe, by the road over the mesa, to Pena Blanca, a deep trail was made, by Indians crossing eastwardly, towards the Pecos. They were on foot, and from the deep permanent trail they made upon the earth, are supposed to have been some two or three hundred. Such a movement bodeth no good.

A month later, the *New Mexican* includes the Governor's message to the Council and House of Representatives in which he states, "It is my disagreeable duty to again report that our Territory still suffers from the hostility of the Indian tribes that surround us [and that] the Navajoes are at this time waging a relentless warfare against our citizens." The governor goes on to assert that the Indians should be "located" to a reservation, "peaceably if possible, forcibly if necessary [as] the white man must see to it that the savages are displaced to make room for him." Indeed, according to the *New Mexican*, in June of 1868, "Lieut. General [William Tecumseh] Sherman of the Indian Commission" negotiated an arrangement with the Navajo "to go upon a reservation in their country, the boundaries of which are clearly defined; they remain thereon, and pursue their pastoral and agricultural avocations; the government agreeing to give annually to each member of the tribe a sum, in wool, or other articles necessary, equal to five dollars, and secure them against the intrusions of whites." It seems that General Sherman, who displaced so many Southerners in his march to the sea during the Civil War, did now relocate other inhabitants to a portion of their ancestral land. However, in an editorial aside, La Farge praises General Sherman's decision as "wise as well as humane," in that it allowed the tribe to flourish and prosper, relatively speaking.

Two months later, though, the newspaper reaffirms its contention that "The Navajoes are a savage and barbarous people," and that those of the tribe that have been pressed into bondage to the whites "possess the advantage of not only religion, but of civilized life," a condition they prefer. "Surely," La Farge comments, "no Southerner ever knew a more touching picture of the benefits of happy, voluntary slavery."

Not all of the dispatches of the *New Mexican* are concerned with the "Indian question." Consider this report from the December 28, 1880, issue of the paper: "The most important arrivals on last night's train were Billy, 'The Kid,' Rudabaugh and Billy Wilson, whom it is unnecessary to introduce to readers of the *New Mexican*." As the story makes clear, "every law-abiding man will be delighted to hear that last night [the famous outlaws] were safely lodged in Santa Fe jail. For this great boon Sheriff Pat Garrett and his posse of brave men are to be thanked." However, a few months later on May 1, 1881, the *New Mexican* reports, "If a shell had hit in Santa Fe yesterday it could have scarcely created more astonishment, or at least more talk, than did the receipt of the news of the Kid's escape from the Lincoln County jail." After evading capture for two months, Billy the Kid is shot and killed by Sheriff Pat Garrett on July 14, 1881. Garrett himself is killed on February 29, 1908, by Wayne Brazil. According to the *New Mexican*,

> The trouble between Garrett and Brazil arose over a lease on Garrett's ranch which Brazil held. They had been quarreling along the road, Garrett being in his buggy and Brazil on horseback. Finally Brazil told Garrett that he wanted to talk to him privately. Garrett got out of the buggy and was shot twice, one shot taking effect in his head and the other entered his chest. He expired in a few minutes.

Of course, the *New Mexican* makes note of other special events in the history of the Territory, as for example, in the January 10, 1887, issue with the headline, "The Last Spike Driven That Unites The Capital Cities Of Colorado And New Mexico," thus allowing rail travel between Santa Fe and Denver. Or consider the June 20, 1910, headline which proclaims, "Santa Fe Is Wild With Joy" over President Taft's signing of the statehood bill.

The newspaper (and hence the book) is full of colorful anecdotes and stories of human curiosity, and I read with interest a column reprinted from February 13, 1888, with the simple title "He Is At Rest." The story begins, "The Most Reverend John Baptist Lamy, for nearly forty years the beloved archbishop of Santa Fe, fell asleep in death at 7:45 o'clock this morning. He passed away as he had lived, calmly and beautifully, a smile of Christian contentment encircling his noble face like a halo of glory." Lamy's life was the the inspiration for Willa Cather's *Death Comes for the Archbishop*, one of my favorite novels and a work that sympathetically treats the Navajo.

Another story of personal interest concerns Nellie Bly, a pioneering woman who was the subject of my daughter's sixth-grade biography project. I remember we were all fascinated learning of the exploits of Nellie Bly, nom de plume of journalist Elizabeth Cochrane, and we were particularly impressed with how she exposed the inhumane conditions of a New York City mental hospital. On January 23, 1890, the *New Mexican* reports,

Nellie Bly, the plucky young woman reporter whom the *New York World* sent out to beat the record of Jules Vernes' creation Phileas Fogg, in his mythical voyage of eighty days around the world, passed Lamy junction on a special train at 11:25 o'clock last night. The little woman was fast asleep, as were Messrs. Hobson and Jennings, editorial writers on the *World*, who met her in San Francisco, on Tuesday.

The column goes on to detail how the run from San Francisco to Chicago promises to be the fastest on record.

Like most small town papers, the *New Mexican* is not immune to "chamber of commerce" moments. The paper regularly extols the virtues of its host town, for example proclaiming on October 8, 1889, that "Santa Fe has more advantages for a residence city than any other town in the southwest," and enumerating these advantages in lush detail. The paper even occasionally runs what we might consider a public service announcement. For example, a column dated October 2, 1895, admonishes

Young men, ye who dally with the innocent-looking cigarette, stand up. Do you know what scientific research has taught the people of this enlightened age about the cigarette? No? Well, here it is revealed by a chemical analysis recently made: The tobacco was found to be strangely impregnated with opium, while the wrapper, which was warranted to be rice paper, was proved to be the most ordinary quality of paper whitened with arsenic. The two poisons combined were present in sufficient quantities to create in the smoker a habit of using opium without his being aware of it, his craving for which can only be satisfied by an incessant consumption of cigarettes.

And, I was amused to read that my hometown of Charlottesville is not the only municipality that has had to wrestle with the role of art in public spaces. "That Bad Woman" is a headline in the October 4, 1950, issue of the *New Mexican*. The corresponding article details that "Miss Fertility, or Mrs. it should probably be, was ordered banished from the wall of the new state office building yesterday because she didn't have any clothes on her plaster limbs and belly. A preacher complained that she was 'suggestive' and down she comes rather than start a row." After poking fun at the guardians of morality, the editors suggest that, "The Fertility panel might be safely replaced by a bas relief pile of manure, a fertility symbol that wouldn't be suggestive of anything but fertility."

Before leaving *Santa Fe: The Autobiography of a Southwestern Town*, let's return to the subject of the Indian. In 1868 the *New Mexican* decrees that the Navajo are a "savage and barbarous people," but a headline from September 6, 1922, characterizes them as "A Marvelous People." Writing about the First Annual Southwest Indian Fair, held in conjunction with the Santa Fe Fiesta, the newspaper asserts

> That the Indians of the Southwest are a most marvelous people is impressed on the writer at the Indian fair as never before. Their art is unique, absolutely distinctive; there is nothing like it in the world; it is a genius for decoration unequaled by any nation of people, inherent and inherited, cropping out, as shown in the exhibits, in the drawing of little children seven and eight years old. This art is one of the world's greatest treasures; it is a priceless possession of America and America is to be congratulated that its value has received final recognition and that every effort will be made by the government and other agencies to foster and preserve and develop it.

Yet in an editorial insertion by La Farge later in the book, he writes that, "Nearly one hundred years after their first mention in the *New Mexican* ... the Navajoes were in the news again." La Farge points out that the Navajo population has exploded, resulting in mass illiteracy and ignorance. But thanks to the efforts of the Navajo-Hopi Rehabilitation Bill, passed during the Eisenhower administration, the situation has improved. Still, the September 27, 1947 *New Mexican* features the following headline: "La Farge Declares Navajoes Exist On Less Than Germans." In the accompanying article, it is reported that according to La Farge, "Navajoes are subsisting on 1,200 calories a day, 300 less than the amount allotted to individuals in Germany [under the Marshall Plan]." In an address to the New Mexican

Association on Indian Affairs, La Farge, according to the article, goes on to say that educational and medical facilities as well as increased opportunities for industrialization are needed to provide "a hope and a possibility."

La Farge concludes *Santa Fe: The Autobiography of a Southwestern Town* by stating, "New Mexico changes, and so does Santa Fe, but neither the state nor its capital has yet entirely lost its old qualities." As evidence, he offers up the story of three young women riding their ponies into the lobby of the La Fonda hotel during the Fiesta of 1958, reminiscent of a similar event nearly 100 years previously. La Farge summarizes the contemporary intrusion with, "The horses behaved admirably and the visitation was well received."

John Pendaries La Farge might take exception to his father's claim that Santa Fe "has [not] yet entirely lost its old qualities." In 2001, the University of New Mexico Press published the younger La Farge's own "autobiography" of the capital city, *Turn Left at the Sleeping Dog: Scripting the Santa Fe Legend, 1920–1955*. The book is dedicated "To my mother, my father, and my grandmother, who together raised me in a most extraordinary environment, one richer in culture, in plural cultures, in personalities, and in eccentricities than most others. Santa Fe may have been the perfect place to have been brought up." Consisting of thirty-six interviews, *Turn Left at the Sleeping Dog*, is an oral history that focuses on an era that La Farge says "saw both a culmination of all that went before it and a birth of new elements, elements that have made the town famous." Indeed, La Farge concludes, the period represents "what many of those who lived there called a 'golden age.'" In the introduction, La Farge comments that the book is not "an academic history" but rather an attempt to preserve the memories of those who lived during this golden age before they passed away. For "in the new millennium," some of the forces that made Santa Fe unique have disappeared. La Farge points in particular to the Indians who confront the tension of preserving their ancient culture while adapting to the demands of contemporary society.

Turn Left at the Sleeping Dog contains two pieces by Oliver La Farge. The first is an excerpt from the January 1931 article in *World's Work* that I referred to earlier in this section. As John Pendaries La Farge acknowledges, this inclusion is not an interview, but rather an "elegant" description. The second piece is an article reprinted from the pages of *The New Yorker* in 1950. Headed

"Department of Amplification," the article is a letter to the editors from Oliver La Farge in Santa Fe dated August 13, 1950. The letter begins:

> Dear Sirs:
>
> Morris Gilbert's description, in *The New Yorker* a few weeks ago, of the terrace on East Ninety-fourth Street, opposite the building in which he lives, struck the well-known responsive chord in me, for here in Santa Fe my wife and I live in a house with French windows looking out on the equivalent of a terrace, and we are of necessity the constant observers of a Santa Fe version of the kind of life Mr. Gilbert observes.

Oliver La Farge goes on to write that "There are three principal social groups to be observed on weekdays; the ball team, the drunks (including much the same cast), and the dogs." In the course of the letter, La Farge describes both notable drunks and dogs, as well as significant dogfights. The article is whimsical, yet stylistically elegant, and it is representative of what I consider to be La Farge's best mode of writing: the self-effacing personal essay, like those rendered so beautifully in *Raw Material*.

There is a long "Postscript" appended to *Turn Left at the Sleeping Dog*, and in it John Pendaries La Farge expresses his frustration at how Santa Fe has changed since the 1950s, a "change [that] has not necessarily been for the better." Particularly, he regrets that, "We are no longer a small town of neighbors." In further delineating the nature of this change, La Farge writes

> From Mexico there comes a strong epithet that is used in northern New Mexico to characterize an offender: *peniche*, which means "mean, spiteful, despicable, vile, low, or nasty." I'm going to turn the word a bit to suit my fancy and use it to characterize a situation and a place. For that is what the City Different [Santa Fe] has become, *peniche*.

La Farge then specifies the ways his hometown has become *peniche*; chief among these, he asserts, the community "has become separated, not just by money and work, but by ethnicity and race." Unfortunately, La Farge concludes, Santa Fe "is becoming like any other city," a realization that clearly saddens this "lifelong citizen" of the capital city. For "Santa Fe has been such a magical place ... This city has had such openness in closed times, such warmth in cold times, such neighborliness in hostile times, such colorful and rich diversity in stodgy and close-minded times, that the loss of these elements, or any part of them, strikes one to the core."

Oliver La Farge was always a disciplined writer, never more so than in his house on College Street in Santa Fe. There he wrote four days a week, from 9:00 a.m. to noon, followed by lunch and a twenty-minute siesta, before again retreating to his study to labor from 2:00 to 5:00 p.m. Yet despite his commitment, La Farge described himself as "the kind of writer who interrupts his work by pacing the floor, emptying ash trays, straightening pictures on the wall or just plain jumping up and down." He could not work with anyone else in the room. Two days a week, La Farge dedicated himself to "Indian business," and in his role as Director of the Association on American Indian Affairs was steadfast in his advocacy during his twenty-plus year tenure in Santa Fe. La Farge essentially believed in the eventual assimilation of Indians into mainstream American society; however, he understood that until then federal protection of native tribes was necessary.

Through his writing and public appearances, La Farge never wavered in bringing the plight of the American Indian into the consciousness of white America. This education often necessitated La Farge detailing the history of abuse, as well as the current reality vis à vis Native Americans and particularly the Navajo. Writing in *Natural History* magazine in 1948, La Farge dispels a prevalent contemporary myth and maintains

> The Navajos do not want to live in relief. They want to support themselves. They are proud, they want to remain Navajos, and as Navajos they want to have true equality with their fellow citizens. They are ready to adapt themselves again, to take into the basic, free pattern of their life new elements of profound change. They can do it and still retain their fundamental values.

Meanwhile, La Farge believes, the Navajos are in danger of losing their manhood. Instead of "feeding every stranger who passes his door, even in dire poverty, devoutly seeking his religious concept of beauty within and without, devoted to his children, a craftsman, an artist, is going day by day, replaced by a cheap actor selling blankets to tourists."

At the time, La Farge saw little possibility of the federal government ameliorating the problems confronting Native Americans. He described the Indian Service as "a repository for individuals not quite able to qualify for parallel positions elsewhere," and believed that the majority of these civil servants were the "social and intellectual inferiors" of the people they ostensibly aided. Writing in *The New Republic*, La Farge decries our government's historic and contemporary treatment of Native Americans:

> For a century and a half our Indian policy could be stated as follows:
>
> Our civilization is *the* civilization. Anything different is savage. Anyway, Indians are inferior. The quicker they become like us the better; they must become Christian, and in so far as the leopard can change his spots, cease to be Indians.
>
> 2. We still need land. Though we do not admit it, we do not intend to let these aborigines retain anything we want. Gold in the Black Hills? Farming land in Kansas? The agent will get the Indians to move, and if he can't do it, the army will.

La Farge later elaborates on this "policy" in a column he wrote in the *New Mexican*. In this piece, he asserts, "The Indians were assaulted, wiped out, broken, besieged, and massacred by hordes of savage white men." He details how the whites, not the Indians, initiated conflict and how the U.S. Army used vastly superior numbers to subdue, indeed decimate, tribes of native people.

In 1956 La Farge published *A Pictorial History of the American Indian*, an exhaustive compendium of North American indigenous life from the Ice Age migration to the reservation system. In the book's last chapter, "The Non-Vanishing American," La Farge assesses the "current" state of the American Indian. He begins the chapter by declaring, "One big fact stands out. The Indians are not vanishing; they are increasing." He maintains that the present day population of federal Indians in the United States proper is 400,000, up from 300,000 at the turn of the century. He goes on to explain the reservation system where Indian country "is subject to federal [not state] law" and "lawsuits arising within it are tried in federal courts." However, "all strong tribes maintain their own police and courts, and jealously guard their right to home rule."

La Farge writes of the many misconceptions regarding the federal government's "care" of Native Americans. For example, he says, "Indians do not get pensions from the government"; in fact, their "rights to relief are the same as anyone else's." In tracing the history of the government's Indian policy, La Farge writes that it changes from "administration to administration." However,

> until 1929 it had a general direction, which was to de-Indianize by breaking up the tribes, destroying tradition, preventing group action, doing everything possible to make it impossible for the Indians to make themselves heard. Along with this went a grim travesty of education, schools that held sick and hungry children to long hours of manual labor, a system of training that had at its highest aim making girls into domestic servants (an occupation Indians with their pride, deeply dislike), boys into farmers and day laborers.

When considering the status of Indians "today," La Farge says "that no general statement about all Indians is wholly correct," but "by and large, they have to an extraordinary degree continued to be Indians ... They have held to the inner quality, to the pride, and to the integrity of their tribes." La Farge further maintains that Native Americans want progress "without loss of identity." However, such progress is threatened by pervasive drinking and systematic poverty. Additionally, "An Indian seeking employment has a tough time. Thin-skinned, proud, shy, and thoroughly uneasy in his new situation, he is readily discouraged, and usually appears stupid and unable to talk."

In conclusion, La Farge writes

> The picture is dreary, but still these remarkable people can drum and sing, joke and laugh—even if some of the jokes now are bitter.

They have not given up. They do not want handouts or charity; they want the guidance and help that is necessary to enable them to help themselves. With a little understanding from their fellow Americans, they still may maintain their goal, which is to be healthy, as competent in all our ways, as active contributors, and solidly self-supporting as the rest of us, and still hold to traditions, generosities, and ancient knowledge that will add greatly to the richness of the American scene.

"Longines Chronoscope: A Television Journal of the Important Issues of the Hour" ran on CBS from 1951 through 1955 every Monday, Wednesday, and Friday from 11:00 to 11:15 p.m. When "distinguished guest" Oliver La Farge, President of the American Association on Indian Affairs, appeared on the program, he was interviewed by members of the CBS news staff and the editorial board of the *New York Times*. The subject at hand involved bills before Congress that would remove federal protection from millions of Indians in a dozen states.

If these bills were to pass, La Farge points out, Indians would face the risk of losing their tax-exempt reservation lands, their access to federal education and health services, and the loss of their sovereign status within reservation boundaries. La Farge's contention prompts one of the panelists to ask, "Why have the Indians isolated themselves? Why haven't they assimilated like more recent immigrants?" (Indians, immigrants?!) La Farge responds that the Indians have not isolated themselves, but that we, the American people, have in fact isolated them. We have conquered them brutally and violently, shown racial discrimination against them, and not prepared them for our manner of operation. As a result, La Farge says, "When they leave the reservations, when they leave their tribes, they usually have very unhappy experiences." When La Farge further maintains that we have never offered the Indians a reasonable education, one interviewer asks him, "Don't they have the same education privileges as the rest of us?" In theory they do, La Farge answers, but he states that fifty percent of school-age Navajo children have no access to educational facilities.

One panelist asks what President Eisenhower was referring to when he suggested the proposed bills would remove second-class status for the Indians.

La Farge indignantly responds, "I don't know what he was referring to except he was ill-informed." The Indian is not a second-class citizen, La Farge asserts; he has all the rights and responsibilities as the rest of us, including the right to vote and the right to engage in military service, which, La Farge says, the Indian has rendered "magnificently."

A panelist next asks, "You said, 'Indians are facing the greatest betrayal of the last 100 years.' What is that betrayal?" This questions leads La Farge to review the provisions of the Allotment Act of 1887: the proposed legislation, he concludes, represents the most serious attack on the rights of the Indian since the founding of the Republic. "Who wants this?" La Farge is asked. In reply, he points out that many reservations are rich in natural resources such as oil, uranium, and timber. Therefore, he ironically says, there are a lot of reasons why it would be convenient to liberate these people so they have no protection and no rights.

When asked, "What do Indians actually want to make them full first-class citizens of the United States?" La Farge answers forcefully and unequivocally: "education." A sound general education would help Indians establish themselves as economically competent and thus better able to earn their own living. The panel suggests that if current federal laws were passed onto the states, the Indians would be provided with desired economic opportunity. La Farge counters with, "They [the states] offer no provision whatsoever," and notes that Indians must have the protection of the federal government until their first class status is guaranteed in practice as in theory.

Time expires at this point, and the host quickly intones, "The opinions expressed were those of the speaker." I find it fascinating to watch this broadcast. La Farge is forceful yet measured throughout, and I relish the way he "schools" the learned panel. Admittedly, at times he comes off as rather stuffy, but maybe that is a by-product of his clipped New England accent and his erect bearing and dapper appearance: his aquiline nose, large-frame glasses, carefully knotted tie, and the handkerchief in the breast pocket of his suit jacket.

It seems safe to say that all of his life Oliver La Farge was in fact concerned about appearances. He believed in certain social amenities and also in doing things the right way. During his years in Santa Fe, La Farge was distressed by the appearance—and the reality—of his estrangement from the children of his first marriage. He even wrote a short story, "The Bright Faces," in which a father confronts the emotional toll of a failed marriage.

Povy, Oliver and Wanden's younger child, had little to with her father during her growing-up years, and she did not ask Oliver to give her away at her 1955 wedding. Perhaps she had good cause not to include him in her nuptials. After the birth of John Pendaries in 1951 and his baptism as a Catholic, Consuelo longed to return to the Church. Father John La Farge, Oliver's uncle and a Roman Catholic priest, was sympathetic to her desire, and he sought to nullify Oliver's marriage to Wanden who strangely agreed to help in this enterprise. Father John "discovered" proof that Wanden was a Roman Catholic who had married outside of her faith, a marriage deemed invalid in the eyes of the Church. (Ironically, though no record of his christening was ever found, Oliver himself was apparently a baptized Catholic. His parents were married in a Catholic ceremony, although Oliver's mother raised him and his siblings as Episcopalians.) Father John appealed to the Bishop of Santa Fe, and the nullification of Oliver and Wanden's marriage was granted. Subsequently, Father John married Oliver and Consuelo in the cathedral in Santa Fe. Povy now considered herself an illegitimate child. Oliver was upset that Povy excluded him from her wedding party, but she had reasoned that asking Oliver to give her away would have been upsetting to her mother. Povy invited Oliver to the wedding, but he chose not to attend.

Born in 1931, Oliver Albee La Farge experienced a tortured relationship with his father. After his parents' divorce in 1937, Oliver lived almost exclusively with his mother, Wanden. Wanden married rancher Andy Kane (who was fifteen years her junior) in 1940, and shortly thereafter young Oliver began referring to himself as Peter, or Pete. Wanden, Andy, and the children lived in Fountain, Colorado, and it appears that Pete did not get along with his stepfather. According to Povy,

> Pete wanted to just ride and run really fast and have fun. He didn't want to go to the livestock auction and sit with Andy and learn the sales ... Pete liked the theory of ranching, but not the reality. He was sensitive, he wrote poetry.

In reality, as a young man Pete was likely suffering from an undiagnosed mental illness—probably schizophrenia—and his erratic and destructive behavior distressed Oliver, who preferred to blame Wanden for their son's problems. Indeed, Pete and his mother often argued, and Oliver believed that Wanden perpetuated lies about him to the children. When troubles surfaced at school for Pete, Oliver wrote to the headmaster and essentially blamed the Kanes for Pete's problems. Oliver could not, or would not, acknowledge that his son's issues might be related to his mental health and not to just poor upbringing.

When the Korean War broke out in 1950, Pete enlisted in the Navy, and Oliver had hopes that military service would provide Pete with much needed direction. Pete listed Oliver, not Wanden, as his next of kin, a designation that Oliver considered "a victory." Pete was assigned to the aircraft carrier *Boxer*, which carried planes and personnel to the war zone and provided air support for the UN forces fighting ashore. In the summer of 1952, a jet crashed while landing on the deck of the *Boxer*, killing nine crewmen on board. Pete was physically uninjured in this incident, but he suffered psychological distress; as a result, he was discharged in February 1953 and sent to Great Lakes U.S. Naval Hospital for psychiatric evaluation. When Pete returned to his mother's ranch, Oliver's hopes for his son soon turned to despair. For his part, in June 1953 Pete wrote letters to his uncles Christopher and Francis La Farge, asking them if he could stay with each until he "could find his bearings." Oliver endorsed this initiative, and was happy that Pete had appealed to his uncles for help. As Oliver confessed to Christopher, "he [Peter] and I are inclined to be over intense together and work each other up. The low, relaxed atmosphere of Rhode Island, and sense of newness and lack of preconceptions, and the enormous spiderweb of family connections and warmth are just the thing."

Much of what I know about Pete I learned from Sandra Hale Schulman's *Don't Tell Me How I Looked Falling: The Ballad of Peter La Farge*, an electronic book published in 2012. This book is a curious compilation of material: a mishmash of oral history, interviews, family photos and letters, and Pete's own writing. Peter's life was indeed a tempestuous one, but it seems worthy of a closer, yet discursive, examination here as he and his father occupied each other's consciousness for three decades.

After Pete's Korean War experience, he managed to get his GED, and he tried to get into college. He asked his former headmaster at Fountain Valley School to intercede on his behalf, but in writing to one college admissions officer in September, 1954, this administrator confesses, "I must say that I consider him [Peter] to be an unstable risk. I am writing this letter to other institutions which may be willing to consider young La Farge further." To Pete, this same headmaster writes, "Pete, I am sure you surmised in not hearing from me that some of the colleges I contacted on your behalf were unable to hold out hope for your admission this fall."

Pete turned to rodeo which he called "a disease, not an occupation." But as he explained, rodeo "eliminates responsibility to a community [and] gives you danger." On the rodeo circuit, Pete initially rode bareback, then saddle broncs. He was a "mugger" in wild horse races, responsible for holding untamed horses while others got the saddle on. Pete was frequently hospitalized with broken bones, and in 1956 he badly hurt his leg in a rodeo accident. During the 1950s, Pete was also an amateur boxer, fighting under the name "Kid Oliver." He won 22 of 24 fights, but twice suffered a broken nose during his pugilistic career.

Late in the 1950s, Peter La Farge pursued acting and writing. He performed in some supporting roles in the Chicago theater scene, and he had a few stunt gigs in movies and television. In 1958 Pete married Suzan Becker, who belonged to the same theater company as he. She was devoted to her husband, and in a letter to her father she proclaimed, "I've finally lost the burning desire to act—and no longer feel the need. Being wife, housekeeper, 'future mother', woman and one character of Suzan B. La Farge are exciting and fulfilling." But in a later missive, dated September 11, 1959, Suzan confesses to her father that she is under psychiatric care, having experienced a mental breakdown and found herself "swimming in unreality." According to Pete's sister Povy, Suzan was admitted to a mental hospital in her home state of Michigan "sometime around 1960 [and] doctors said she couldn't be cured." By this time, Pete was living alone in New York City, but because he had been baptized a Catholic after marrying Suzan, he could not divorce her or, as his father had done with his mother, annul the marriage. Suzan died on November 30, 1977. According to her death certificate, Suzan was "hanging onto a moving car and fell on the road at 11:20 a.m." It is apparently unknown if her death was an accident, a homicide, or a suicide.

Encouraged by folksinger Cisco Houston, Pete turned to singing and songwriting, and he soon became a fixture in the Greenwich Village music scene. He caught the eye of young Bob Dylan, who later said of La Farge:

> Pete is one of the unsung heroes of the day. His style was just a little bit too erratic. But it wasn't his fault, he was always hurting and having to overcome it ... When I think of a guitar poet or protest singer, I always think of Peter, but he was a love song writer too.

Dylan's girlfriend at the time was Suze Rotolo, who appears with her boyfriend on the cover of the album "The Freewheeling Bob Dylan." She said of Peter,

> I was very young when I first met Bob's friend Peter La Farge, but the first thing you remember was how gorgeous he was, very handsome. I remember how he looked with his black hair pulled back and striding into a room wearing a black cape with red lining, very handsome, very striking, just strode into a room, very serious, that's what I remember most.

Like many people, Suze Rotolo believed that Peter La Farge was a Native American, a misconception he did little to correct.

In September, 1962, Pete Seeger hosted a "hootenanny" at Carnegie Hall intended to introduce new musical talent. Dylan sang La Farge's "As Long as the Grass Shall Grow" at this event; this exposure and La Farge's own performances in Greenwich Village landed him a recording contract with Folkways Records, and over the next four years, La Farge recorded five albums for the label. Most of the songs on these albums focused on Native American themes, including the haunting "The Ballad of Ira Hayes," which tells the story of the Pima Indian who helped raise the American flag at the World War II battle at Iwo Jima. During these years, Peter lived with Inger Marie Nielsen, a former Playboy bunny originally from Denmark. Peter's mother Wanden essentially subsidized Peter in New York. She paid all his bills and even set up a charge account for Inger at B. Altman's. Again, according to Peter's sister Povy, Wanden harbored a lot of guilt regarding Peter, and she regretted that her husband Andy so disliked his stepson. But when in the winter of 1964 Inger gave birth to her and Peter's daughter, Karen, Wanden took the baby away when Karen was only two weeks old. Karen's subsequent life was a history of disasters, and like her mother, she was diagnosed as a paranoid schizophrenic. Inger lived for many years after the death of Peter, who "she loved with all her heart."

In 1963, Johnny Cash performed at Carnegie Hall in a concert meant to be recorded by Columbia Records. At the time, Cash was wasted on drugs and suffering from anxiety and an inability to sleep. He went "off script" at the concert and the recording equipment was turned off. After the show, Cash traveled to Greenwich Village with folksinger Ed McCurdy, who introduced Cash to Peter La Farge. Cash was familiar with "The Ballad of Ira Hayes," and he told La Farge he wanted to record the song one day. Cash saw the song as a vehicle that expressed the plight of modern Indians, and he wanted the ballad to be the foundation of an entire album. Cash even visited the mother of the deceased Ira Hayes at her home on a Pima reservation in Arizona, and she gave the singer a small black stone, an Apache tear, which Cash wore around his neck when he did record the song in early March 1964. Cash invited La Farge to attend this recording session in Nashville, and as one Cash biographer writes,

> It was easy to see why Cash and La Farge would connect. They were about the same age (La Farge was a year older), shared an empathy with Native Americans, and they viewed music as their life's mission, a validation. They also shared a restless, illicit substance-fueled wild streak that made observers fear they could both self-destruct.

Indeed, as Cash later wrote of La Farge in his autobiography, "His voice was a voice crying in the wilderness. I felt lucky to be hearing it. Peter was great. He wasn't careful with the Thorazine though." Also, Johnny Cash was never fully cognizant of Peter La Farge's family history, believing, as many did, that his friend was a Native American. As he said of La Farge, "Peter was very proud of his heritage and he was adamant about the wrongs that his people had suffered over the years."

Released on October 1, 1964, Johnny Cash's album "Bitter Tears: Ballads of the American Indians" included four other La Farge songs in addition to "Ira Hayes": "As Long as the Grass Shall Grow" is critical of American presidents for breaking treaties with Native Americans, while "Drums" is a salute to Indian culture. "White Girl" details the prejudice that hinders Anglo/Indian relationships, and "Custer" is a savage portrait of a general extolled in the history texts and in popular imagination. Cash had a lot of anxiety regarding the "Bitter Tears" project. According to his bass player at the time, you can see the stress that Cash was feeling in the photo of the album cover. "Look at it closely," he said. "Look at his face, skin, bones, his elbow; that's what we're dealing with." "Bitter Tears" eventually sold 100,000 copies, and it was nominated for a Grammy in the Best Country and Western Album category. It was selected by the Library of Congress as "truly representative of American Indians," and it certainly enhanced Cash's reputation for creativity and innovation.

When it was released as a single in the summer of 1964, "The Ballad of Ira Hayes" was not embraced by the country music establishment, who wondered why Cash was speaking so vehemently for Native Americans and therefore, as the logic went, criticizing American values. Despite the fact that many disc jockeys refused to play the 45, it nonetheless climbed to number three on the country charts. Still, Cash was infuriated by Nashville's response to the song, and as a result, he placed a full-paged in *Billboard*, in which he asked,

> DJs, station managers, owners, etc., where are your guts? I'm not afraid to sing the hard bitter lines that the son of Oliver La Farge wrote ... Teenage girls and Beatles record buyers don't want to hear this sad story of Ira Hayes—but who cries more easily, and who always goes to sad movies to cry??? Teenage girls.

Cash goes on to challenge those in charge of radio stations to listen to the song again, pointing out that it is "gutless to say it is not a country song … The Ballad of Ira Hayes' is "strong medicine," he concludes, but "so is Rochester—Harlem—Birmingham and Vietnam … I had to fight back when I realized that so many are afraid of 'Ira Hayes.' Just one question: Why???"

⋘

A quick check of Spotify reveals over a dozen versions of "The Ballad of Ira Hayes," not including the releases of Peter La Farge and Johnny Cash. Among the artists who have recorded the song are Bob Dylan, Kris Kristofferson, Kinky Friedman, and Appalachian folksinger Hazel Dickens. As mentioned earlier, Ira Hayes helped raise the American flag atop Mt. Suribachi in the World War II battle for the island of Iwo Jima. But who, exactly, is Ira Hayes, and why is his tragic story so compelling? To answer these questions, we must turn to *Flags of Our Fathers*, the riveting biography of the six "flag raisers" by James Bradley (with Ron Powers). As Bradley writes in the beginning of his book,

> Something unusual happened to these six: History turned all its focus, for 1/400th of a second, on them. It froze them in an elegant instant of battle: froze them in a camera lens as they hoisted an American flag on a makeshift pole. Their collective image, blurred and indistinct yet unforgettable, became the most recognized, the most reproduced in the history of photography. It gave them a kind of immortality—a faceless immortality. The flag raising on Iwo Jima became a symbol of the island, the mountain, the battle; of World War II; of the highest ideals of the nation, of valor incarnate. It became everything except the salvation of the boys who formed it.

In the photograph, Hayes is the last figure on the left, his hands not quite reaching the pole. He is different, apart from the rest, and his position is a metaphor for the misunderstood and solitary nature of his life.

Hayes was raised on a Pima reservation in Arizona in a culture that valued quiet, self-effacing behavior. Ira attended elementary school on the reservation before he enrolled as a boarding student at the Phoenix Indian School, where he didn't mix well with students from other tribes. He enlisted in the Marines after Pearl Harbor; he was nineteen years old, and before his departure for boot camp, his community held a feast in his honor with jackrabbit stew, spicy tortillas, fried potatoes, wild spinach, and bean pudding. Hayes earned his USMC Paratrooper wings on November 30, 1942, the first Pima to graduate from parachute training. He saw action in the South Pacific at Bougainville where he had landed on December 3, 1943. Hayes was deeply affected by the fierce hand-to-hand combat with the camouflaged enemy in the thick jungle, and when he returned home on leave, his mother thought he looked old and solemn. After further training at Camp Pendleton in California and at Hawaii's Camp Tarawa, Ira and comrades from Easy Company readied for the assault on Iwo Jima, where the Japanese were entrenched in caves and concrete bunkers. As Bradley writes, the Americans

> were about to enter a battle against an underground enemy that had endured the Pacific's most intense bombing of World War II and had not been disturbed. The only way the cave Kamikaze could be overcome was by direct frontal assault, young American boys walking straight into Japanese fields of fire.
>
> It would be a battle pitting American flesh against Japanese concrete.

At first, "Japanese concrete" seemed to be winning, as the initial day's casualties were staggering: 556 American troops killed "ashore and afloat," and approximately 1,800 others wounded. Ninety-nine soldiers experienced combat fatigue.

In subsequent days, the Marines continued to advance against an unseen enemy, and the casualties continued to mount: by the end of the third day of battle official records reported 644 killed, 4,168 wounded, and 560 unaccounted for. On the fifth day, the 3rd Platoon took control of the summit of Mt. Suribachi, where Associated Press photographer Joe Rosenthal, in a moment of true serendipity, captured the flag-raising moment. His photo was published in Sunday newspapers around the country on February 25, 1945. President Roosevelt immediately ordered to Washington the "6 enlisted men and/or officers who actually appear in the Rosenthal photograph of flag raising at Mount Suribachi." Roosevelt intended to send these six soldiers on a bond tour to raise money for the war effort. But three of the six flag raisers had died in fighting in the interval between the conquest of Mount Suribachi and the publication of the photo. Rene Gagnon was the only living soldier from the photograph identified by his superiors. Hayes knew he was in the photograph as well, but he had no desire to leave his fellow soldiers still on the island. He swore Gagnon to secrecy, and once in D.C., Gagnon identified the flag raisers as himself, John Bradley, and the deceased Michael Strank, Franklin Sousley, and Hank Hansen. (Ironically, it was later determined that Hank Hansen, John Bradley, and most recently, Rene Gagnon himself, did not participate in the raising of the flag.) When Gagnon was ordered to reveal the sixth man, he gave up Ira's name and Hayes was flown to Washington on April 15. There he spotted an error in the caption of the photo. and told the Marine PR officer assigned to him that Harlon Block, not Hank Hansen, helped to raise the flag. The officer told Hayes to keep quiet, as it was too late to make the change.

Gagnon, Bradley, and Hayes were met by frenzied crowds of hero worshippers wherever they went. In Washington, they were feted by Congress and attended the season opener between the Yankees and the Senators. Hayes was uncomfortable with this acclaim, repeating insistently that the real heroes had died on Iwo Jima. Increasingly he took refuge in the bottle, and his handler struggled to keep Ira presentable and responsive. The news media regarded Ira with curiosity and emphasized his "Indianness." The night before a massive Sunday rally at Chicago's Soldier Field, Ira went missing and after a night of intense drinking, he was found by the local police. They rushed him back to his hotel, where he was doused with ice water and "slapped him into something resembling sobriety an hour before the ceremony." Ira was sent back overseas to stop his embarrassing behavior, but the Bond Tour had proven to be a big success. As America closed out the War in the Pacific, $26.3 billion dollars, nearly double the goal, was pledged for this effort.

After the war, Ira moved back to the reservation, where he took on a number of menial jobs. He carried an American flag in his back pocket to use as a prop when approached by tourists for a photograph. He refused to talk about Iwo Jima and he drank heavily, resulting in multiple arrests for drunk and disorderly conduct. He hitchhiked 1,300 miles in three days to find Harlon Block's family and inform them that Harlon was in the Rosenthal photo. Harlon's mother pursued redress and the wrong was eventually righted.

Filled with remorse and self-pity, Ira's drinking and arrests grew commonplace. He moved to Chicago to work at the International Harvester plant, but in September, 1953, the *Chicago Sun Times* ran a picture of Ira behind bars with the headline "Iwo Flagraiser Jailed As Drunk." Ira returned to Arizona in November and a year later he was on hand at Arlington National Cemetery for the dedication of the Iwo Jima Memorial, the world's tallest bronze statue. When the statue was unveiled, Bradley writes, "Ira beheld the image, burst into tears, and buried his face in Goldie's [mother of Franklin Sousley] lap." A week before Christmas 1954, Ira was arrested for the fifty-first time for being drunk and disorderly, and "on the frigid morning of January 24, 1955—one month shy of ten years since he raised a flag—Ira was found dead at the age of thirty-two." His body was discovered lying facedown in a pool of his own vomit and blood; the coroner ruled his death accidental due to overexposure to the freezing weather and too much alcohol. Thousands mourned his loss by visiting his body as it lay in state in the Arizona Capitol Rotunda before burial at Arlington National Cemetery.

In 1961, Universal Pictures released a somewhat sanitized biopic of Ira Hayes's life called *The Outsider*. According to the Turner Classic Movies introduction to the film, "the choice of the leading man caused disbelief and derision" as Tony Curtis, "a Jewish kid from the Bronx" was picked to betray a Native American from Arizona. The film begins with Ira's enlistment; his mother tells him, "I know you are going to be a good Marine, but don't forget to be a good Pima boy and go to church." In boot camp, Ira receives the nickname "Chief," and is looked after by a fellow recruit played by James Franciscus. (In the "it's a small world" category, in real life Franciscus was the cousin of Suzan Becker, wife of Peter La Farge.) On liberty in San Diego, Ira's buddies raise a toast to "Pocahontas, the Indian on the nickel, the Marines."

Ira comments that he has "never had a drink" and that he's "afraid" of alcohol. Of course, in reality this is untrue, as Ira had been twice arrested for drunk and disorderly conduct before his enlistment.

The action shifts to Iwo Jima, and one scene features Ira's philosophical rumination on the nature of death. When Ira is recruited for the flag raising, he initially protests saying, "I hate to have my picture taken." The photo then appears on the front page of newspapers around the country, and the White House orders the depicted survivors to the nation's capital. In the film, Hayes is sent to Washington with Gagnon, another deviation from the true story. Ira drinks heavily on the subsequent Bond Tour, and when he is sent back to combat duty, a general scolds him, "You're a public figure now. You don't belong to yourself anymore."

Ira returns home after the war, and, according to the film, he is selected by the Pima to go to Washington and advocate for tribal water rights. In another perversion of the facts, Ira gets drunk and is arrested, and his jail cell photo is splashed all over the papers. However, as we have seen, this embarrassing episode took place in Chicago, not D.C. Ira loses the faith of his tribe, and he declares, "I ain't been the same since they [the government] tried to make me something I ain't." Largely through newsreel footage, the film does depict the dedication of the Iwo Jima Memorial. On the night after the ceremony, Ira, alone, prays at the base of the bronze monolith, "I promise I will make it. I promise myself. I promise you. I promise. I promise." Back at home, Ira seems cleansed of his burden. He forswears drinking (again, not an accurate representation), and he seeks redemption by working hard on behalf of his neighbors and fellow tribespeople. But when he is not nominated to the tribal council, Ira goes on a drinking binge and, haunted by memories of his past, dies on a clumsily artificial set, his arms outstretched in a pose reminiscent of his position during the flag raising. It's a very "Hollywood ending" to a not good movie, but the film, like Peter La Farge's eponymous ballad, did much to mythologize Ira Hayes.

It makes sense that Peter La Farge would be drawn to the doomed life of Ira Hayes. Both men were indeed outsiders who struggled with addiction and what we would today deem post-traumatic stress syndrome. In the song, Hayes is misused and abandoned by the military, and in Hayes, Pete also saw a symbol of government malfeasance towards Native Americans. The Pima

Indians had been victimized by government neglect like so many other tribes suffering the effects of broken treaties. The song is political, a protest designed to raise awareness, and to that end Peter La Farge sang "Ira Hayes" at the 1963 Newport Folk Festival while the Albuquerque Inter-Tribal Dancers performed on stage alongside him. Johnny Cash's success with "Bitter Tears" in 1964 led Columbia Records to sign La Farge as a country artist in the fall of 1965. But on October 27, 1965, less than two months after La Farge's mother Wanden took Peter and Inger's daughter, Inger found Peter dead of an apparent overdose in their apartment at The Dakota.

In a January 1966 obituary in *Sing Out* magazine, critic Julius Lester wrote of La Farge, "He is beyond us—the audiences that never quite understood him, and the friends who pitied him ... None of them can hurt him anymore ... Their tongues and pens can no longer hurt one that was too gentle to retaliate and strong enough to resist." Pete was buried on his mother's ranch in Colorado; Inger died in September, 2010 in a mental health facility in Denmark. As of this writing, their daughter Karen is institutionalized in Colorado.

One of the "friends who pitied" Peter La Farge was Beat Generation writer Seymour Krim, who himself died from an overdose of barbiturates in 1989. Krim wrote an essay about Peter titled "Son of Laughing Boy" which was first published in 1973 in *London Magazine* and later in Krim's anthology of essays, *you & me*, a "book of a guy who's withdrawn from some of the public action of the 60s into the simplest kind of affection or despair in his relations with others."

"Son of Laughing Boy" begins with the following observation:

> The last clear, definite, stamped, everlasting picture of Peter La Farge that I hold in my brain has him in cowboy drag slouching down the steps of a small with-it (*Times Book Review* people, actors) restaurant in the West 40s, tears oozing down his cheeks from the contact lenses he thought would make him look like Randolph Scott forever stalking Laredo ... [I] said to myself a little self righteously but with a pang in my heart that I'd never admit: You poor fucking star-shooter. You think this masquerade can go on forever. Well, baby, it can't. Nay.

"Less than six months later," Krim writes, [La Farge] was dead."

Krim then traces his relationship with Peter and confesses, "I had love for Pete La Farge and, although I couldn't admit it at the time, it was probably what we call homosexual love." He describes how Peter vacillated between two roles; he had "the tall, muscular, battered body of a cowboy and the straight black hair and olive-skinned face of what could be an Indian." Krim says of Peter that, "he wanted to be a hundred marvelous shimmering things in the air ... but in the end he was forced back to his bones like all of us." Krim maintains that Peter fabricated a "mod hero" image, and took seriously this masquerade, which necessitated "thumbing his nose" at his birth class and reinventing himself.

> Yet there was something fantastically, challengingly beautiful as well as doomed about Pete's bid to become his own impossible hero. He had come out of the Southwest, the son of Oliver Lafarge [sic], the Harvard man who had brought the Navajo into American life with *Laughing Boy* in 1930 ... Peter never got on with his Great White Father ... he was practically a non-son after the old man birthed him and in fact named him Oliver, Jr. with a cool, arrogant eye for the future of his little carbon copy which included a New England church school and Harvard.

Throughout the essay, as the above suggests, Krim is unstinting in his disdain for Oliver La Farge. He says that La Farge "could only plot with inspiration over a bottle," and calls him "the proud and sterile don of Southwest fiction." He goes on to claim that "the older La Farge made notes on the Indians he wrote about from a proper distance, like a cartoon of the Harvard anthropologist that he actually was when he first came to the Southwest in the 20s." He casts Oliver and Peter's struggles as "oedipal," resulting in "the son finally admitting that he saw his father in him and the father bowing his imperial head to the reality that he too is in his wild son." It is clear Oliver was confused by Peter, but he had a begrudging pride in him nonetheless. As Krim writes, Oliver remarks in his liner notes for Pete's Columbia album *Peter La Farge* that, "It still bewilders me to have this turn up in my family, but it's a proud bewilderment."

On July 24, 1963, Oliver La Farge entered Bataan Hospital in Santa Fe, the same hospital where six years previously he had undergone a lung resection. Now he had a second lung operation performed, but the stress proved too great for his weakened heart. He died at 3:00 p. m. on Friday, August 2. Because of his intense dislike of the Catholic Church, La Farge had stipulated that he was to be laid to rest in an Episcopal service; this demand, of course, was a blow to Consuelo. The funeral took place at Santa Fe's Episcopal Church of the Holy Faith on Monday, August 5, and was attended by many Indians from Taos Pueblo. He was buried with military honors at the National Cemetery in Santa Fe, and his pall bearers included the Secretary of the Interior, the Commissioner of Indian Affairs, a Pulitzer-Prize winning author, and representatives of many tribes.

While La Farge believed in God, he maintained a pantheistic understanding of man as subject to the forces of nature. He appreciated the Navajo concept of "hozhoni," a state of spiritual peace reached through prayers, dancing, song, and art. As he wrote in *Raw Material*, "I did not become a convert to the Navajo religion, but it showed me the way out of desolation." In the same essay, he comments on the nature of his faith as follows:

> What my creed finally came to be is not important, it represents simply one individual's private groping for God. I doubt that I, Oliver La Farge, that inner essence of individuality, that spark distinct from all other sparks to which we cling so desperately and without which it is difficult even to imagine a universe in existence, the centre and self which we denote so aptly by the single, narrow, upright stride of a capital I, will continue as such. The loss of that belief is the loss of one of the greatest comforts of religion, it makes it a little more difficult to face growing old and to contemplate death. The answer to it is to contemplate and become accustomed to the idea of the extinction of the ego, hand in hand with contemplating the nature of God. This can be done, although it does not come easy to a full-living, sinful white man.

On August 3, 1963, *The New York Times* published a front-page obituary for Oliver La Farge under the headline "Oliver La Farge Is Dead at 61; Author Helped Indians' Cause." The obituary notes that "Mr. La Farge's tireless efforts spurred private and public projects to improve the Indian's welfare and assure his social, civil, and constitutional rights." In fact, the article states, La Farge was "revered" by Indians who often viewed him as "their last recourse in their fight for survival." Mention is made of La Farge's prominent family, and that its roots can be traced from Benjamin Franklin. His early life and education is detailed, as is his career as an anthropologist and his service in World War II. He is described as a "practical man with balanced judgment" who asserted that "The Indian as I have met him is fine, brave, loyal, and intelligent. He is skillful and has artistic sensibility. He is patiently industrious about work which interests him and maintains a high level of craftsmanship."

The remembrance insists that La Farge "deplored paternalism," quoting his assertion that "More responsibility and authority must be turned over to the Indians themselves, leading them on until they can take care of their own future entirely in their own hands." After his father's death, Peter La Farge held a tribute concert for Oliver at Town Hall in the fall of 1963. Pete had previously hosted other concerts at Town Hall, but they were financial failures because, as Seymour Krim, succinctly writes, "Pete could hardly organize his trips to the john at this point." Peter wrote the following incantatory dedication in the booklet for his father's tribute:

> Oliver La Farge is a name like a flag;
> He wove the chiefs blankets of his stories
> From all four directions
> Boxing the compass of inspiration
> He held seldom beauty by the hand
> It swarms along his lines
> The flint and steel of truth
> Light constant sparks among his words.
> Tall cliff dweller
> The Indians called him.
> He sailed the cause of Indian rights upon his heart,

Challenging the iron fingernail of greed
He held open the awful gates of endings
Swinging shut upon the tribes
His soul sore from shattered treaties
In the dark of Washington
The Warrior is gone.
The war pony has no rider
There are no more words to be enchanted
He rose up from illness
To speak to Taos Pueblo
And the bitter knight of ink
Will joust no more
The Indian fight
Must have worn a cavity in his heart
But he never showed it.
Indians blanketed,
Their long hair trussed
Carried the coffin
To its deliberate rest.
He was a seldom man.

So, what is the legacy today of Oliver La Farge, this "seldom man"? As I have already mentioned, La Farge's life was a paradoxical one, and his place in our literary landscape is, as critic Paul Engle wrote, "curious." We have seen that the subject of his writing was generally alien to his upbringing. He lived, spiritually and intellectually, among a forgotten people, and brought their special challenges into the consciousness of the American public. For over half his life he fought for the welfare of the American Indian, a fight that was inevitably fraught with frustration. La Farge was the first author to write realistically about the Navajo, and he presented their world accurately and without sentimentality.

La Farge was a skillful writer, whose work is characterized by grace and clarity. As one critic states, "La Farge professed to apply constant judgment as he wrote, examining each sentence, phrase, word, checking frequently to ensure consistency in his characters and in relations among them." As a writer, La Farge possessed a great ear for the rhythm of language. His understanding of Navajo speech and dialect imbued his style of writing. He grasped the polite nature of conversation between two Indians, as in the scene with Laughing Boy and his uncle when Slim Girl's past is revealed. Finally, as we have discussed, La Farge had the great ability to present Native American life in terms appreciated by Anglo readers, terms that engender understanding and empathy. As corroboration, consider this quote from *Time* magazine on August 26, 1935:

> With the novels of Oliver La Farge, braves and squaws seem at last to be given sensible speaking parts, emerging as complex, poetic, dignified, good-humored men and women deeply conscious of the evil times that have come upon their race. Never loquacious, they speak with an easy formality that has the charm of a good translation of dialect ... La Farge's stories ... have the distinction of making Indian rites and traditions seem as human and amiable as college proms or midwestern barn dances.

It seems fair to say that La Farge's novels and short stories are very much influenced by his training as an anthropologist and linguist, in that much of his fiction deals with societies in transition and man's role in these changing environments. His background as a scientist afforded him experiences that allowed him to expand the conservative views of his upbringing to become a sympathetic renderer of Native American history and culture. Indeed, the two novels of La Farge that have had lasting impact are the two that portray Navajo life, *Laughing Boy* and *The Enemy Gods*, books that brought Indians "into the consciousness of Americans as something other than casual savages without tradition or style." La Farge broke away from the literary traditions of such writers as James Fenimore Cooper, and in doing so, he greatly influenced those who followed him. As one critic writes,

> A comparison of La Farge with the most distinguished of his successors, all of them contributors to the Native American

Renaissance, shows that while he may not have had the last word in the field of Indian fiction, he had one of the first and most enduring voices, one that is still worth listening to, if only for its echo.

La Farge biographer Robert A. Hecht writes that "Oliver La Farge was not a great man." In fact, Hecht insists, La Farge was not particularly "moral" except when it came to his relations with the Indians. His drinking, his marital infidelities to Wanden, and his practical abandonment of Peter and Povy suggest that he was far from content. He was often cynical and sarcastic, and as one acquaintance said, "He was not a kind man, he was a tough and salty one, not always easy to get along with and very hard to please." But as Hecht concludes, "He did have genius in him." In his biography *Indian Man*, however, D'Arcy McNickle asserts that "La Farge possessed an extraordinary capacity for entering into warm and enduring relationships, sharing himself deeply and unreservedly, and being himself renewed by personal attachments." McNickle does concede that, "the fact that [La Farge] never repeated the success of *Laughing Boy*, and that strangers knew him as the author of only one book, whipped up inner storms." McNickle goes on to say that

> His failure to grow in stature, or at least in public recognition, brought not only disappointment but a chastened outlook which he was willing to reveal publicly. He chose the Twenty-Fifth Anniversary Report of the Harvard Class of 1924 to acknowledge his discomfiture. He wrote of "the slow but relentless arrival of the realization that … one will never be great" as a writer. "The dream one had at the beginning," he confessed, "is achingly real, but it will never be fulfilled."

In conclusion, Oliver Hazard Perry La Farge was a man of deep conviction and inner turmoil. While he was an indifferent father to Povy and Peter, he lavished affection on John Pendaries and actively participated in his upbringing. La Farge was an unstinting, tireless advocate for the rights of Native Americans, and his attitude regarding the "Indian problem" evolved over time. He was an uncommonly fine writer who, in my opinion, did fulfill the promise he experienced with the early success of *Laughing Boy*. He was both imaginative and exacting, and took justifiable pride in his ability as a craftsman.

Finally, I confess that I found great pleasure in learning about Oliver La Farge and his prominent family. The history of the La Farges seems a microcosm of the American story. From the distinguished lineage of Oliver's mother to the self-made success of his paternal French immigrant ancestors, Oliver's family experienced the best that our country has to offer, and they fulfilled its promise. Oliver's own personal triumphs and failures also seem uniquely American. The burden of class, the dysfunctional first marriage, the associated tragedy of mental health issues and addiction experienced by Peter, and the "cross ethnic" marriage to Consuelo, flesh out many themes associated with 20th century American life.

My journey into the life and work of Oliver La Farge has been—and continues to be—a deeply enriching sojourn. During this pilgrimage, I have learned so much about anthropology, Native American life, and the Southwest, all previously foreign realms to me. While I'm not sure I would want Oliver La Farge as a friend, I am indeed very grateful that I have made his acquaintance.

AFTERWORD

I BEGAN THIS BOOK BY DETAILING MY EDUCATION—OR LACK thereof—on matters of Native American history and culture. During the course of this volume, I have attempted to explore this history and culture, primarily, of course, through the works of Oliver La Farge. It is now my intention to briefly examine some other, largely contemporary works of Native American fiction and nonfiction and briefly compare the themes they raise with the ideas that permeate La Farge's own writing. This investigation certainly will not be an exhaustive one, but more a general perusal of Native American literature as I understand it.

First, however, we must consider what, exactly, constitutes Native American literature. For example, does a so-called Native American novel have to be written by one who is an Indian?

Perhaps not, says David Treuer in *Native American Fiction: A User's Manual*, where the author writes that "the sentiment (and it is a sentiment) that Native American literature should be defined by the ethnicity of its producers (more so than defined by anything else) says more about politics and identity than it does about literature." I am comforted by these words in a time when the debate over cultural appropriation in literature burns hotly. As Treuer goes on to write

> My argument is not about how Native American fiction is created.
> I am concerned about how it is read; how we ... walk toward it. To
> interpret and critique Native American fiction successfully I suspect

we need both our moccasins and our hobnails, our buckskin vests and leather jerkins. To see Native American literature as linked with American literature; to see culture as an active character in modern novels (much in the same way as haunted houses are in Romances) instead of reading novels *as culture*, that is, as products of difference rather than attempts to create it; to see things this way makes our criticism and our novels richer.

So here I go in my hobnail boots and leather jerkin to "walk toward" Native American fiction. Won't you come along, too?

I first read Louise Erdrich's novel *Love Medicine* shortly after its 1984 publication. I was blown away by the story, the depiction of reservation life, and the desperate search for identity which the characters conducted. *Love Medicine*'s non-linear format features first-person and third-person limited narrators—three women and four men—that span four generations from the 1930s to the 1980s. These narrators primarily focus on the complicated relationships of the Kashpaw and Lamartine families, especially the matriarchs of these respective clans. Indeed, Marie Kashpaw and Lulu Lamartine are family-oriented providers and nurturers as well as rivals for the affections of Nector Kashpaw, Marie's husband and Lulu's lover.

These two women are at the core of the novel; they are strong and confident in who they are, and they loom large over the trajectory of the novel's plot. Yet they are full of human weaknesses and foibles; as Marie's granddaughter, Albertine, says of her,

> When I was very young, she always seemed the same size to me as the rock cairns commemorating Indian defeats around here. But every time I saw her now I realized that she wasn't so large, it was just that figure was weathered and massive as a statue roughed out of rock.

Marie believes in herself, even as she acknowledges her husband's affair with Lulu and the possibility that she might lose Nector to her rival. However, as Marie explains, "I'd still be Marie. Marie. Star of the Sea! I'd shine when they stripped off the wax!"

Lulu Lamartine is also a self-possessed woman. She is reckless with men, but she is a good caretaker of their offspring. "A woman of detachable parts," she manages her children, all boys, with strength and affection. Lulu is unapologetic about who she is. As she says,

> And so when they tell you that I was heartless, a shameless man-chaser, don't ever forget this: I loved what I saw. And yes, it is true that I've done all the things they say. That's what gets them. What aggravates them is I've never shed one solitary tear. I'm not sorry. That's unnatural. As we all know, a woman is supposed to cry.

Love Medicine is a rich and arresting work that echoes many of the motifs of Oliver La Farge's fiction, including the bleakness of reservation existence, the destructive effects of alcohol, and the pervasive sense of humor that characterizes Native American life. Erdrich's multilayered family saga and its unblinking view of twentieth century Native American life make her novel a work of genuine artistry and achievement.

Author Tommy Orange considers *Love Medicine* a "formative book" that deeply influenced his own writing. In a *Washington Post* article dated November 21, 2018, Orange proclaims,

> The writing in this book, which follows many different people, families, and experiences, is so strong and distinct. It walks the reader through so many kinds of voices in a world that, at the time it came out, so few people knew or understood. It brings to light something wholly new about a people trying to grapple with a kind of life more Americans should absolutely try to understand.

Ten years after its publication, I included *Love Medicine* in the curriculum of the Advanced Placement (AP) English Literature class I taught at Charlottesville High School. One of the students in that class was Ben Railton, one of the brightest kids I've taught in my thirty-five years in the classroom. (I'm not sure I taught Ben as much as he taught me.) At age 17, Ben was a perceptive reader who succinctly—and, it appeared, effortlessly—articulated his insights into the literature we studied. To prepare for the AP exam, students wrote lots of sample essays, and Ben's essays, I remember, seemed practically flawless. I can still recall how in one such paper, Ben took a very minor scene from *The Sound and the Fury* and in two short pages demonstrated how that scene encapsulated the varied themes of Faulkner's novel.

Backtrack another twenty years. In the fall of 1974, in my second year at the University of Virginia, I enrolled in an English class on the literature of the American Renaissance, my first real exposure to Emerson, Thoreau, and Hawthorne, now among my most treasured acquaintances. I believe we even read (or at least we were assigned to read) Melville's *Moby Dick*. The class was taught by Professor Stephen Railton, a freshly-minted Ph.D. from Columbia who with his wife Ilene had arrived in Charlottesville in the summer of 1974. While I did little in this class to distinguish myself, it did foster my desire to declare English as my major, a path of study that opened up new worlds to me, worlds found between the covers of books. Professor Railton retired from the University in the spring of 2019 after forty-five years of classroom teaching. However, he created and continues to direct Digital Yoknapatawpha, "a collaboration between an international team of Faulkner scholars and technologists at the University of Virginia."

So what happened to Ben? Well, after graduating from Charlottesville High School he went to Harvard and then earned a Ph.D. in English from Temple University. Today, Ben is Professor of English Studies and Coordinator of American Studies at Fitchburg State University. He writes the daily *AmericanStudier* public scholarly blog and a biweekly column for the *Saturday Evening Post*. I'm a great admirer of Ben's blog, and over the years we have managed to stay in touch; occasionally we get together when he brings his two boys to visit their grandparents Steve and Ilene in Charlottesville.

In 2007, the University of Alabama Press published Ben's first book, *Contesting the Past, Reconstructing the Nation: American Literature and Culture in the Gilded Age, 1876–1893*. The second chapter of this volume is titled "If We Had Known How to Write, We Would Have Put All These Things Down and They Would Not Have Been Forgotten: 'Silenced Voices, Forgotten Histories, and the Indian Question.'" In this chapter, Ben examines "how the myth of the West underwent a significant shift over the course of the nineteenth century," a shift that resulted in an attempt to erase Native American voices from the "Western narrative." Native Americans, Ben argues, were seen as obstacles for the "settling and 'civilizing' of the West." Ben points out that even friends of the Indians espoused assimilation, a process that would, if successful, have ensured "the disappearance of Indian language and traditions." Ben then goes on to examine five literary works of the era, four by white writers and one by a Native American. Two of the books, Bret Harte's novella *In the Carquinez Woods* and Joaquin Miller's *Shadows of Shasta*, feature Native American narrators attempting "to narrate their identities and histories as well as their connections to white society." But these narrators "are ultimately silenced and lost." Conversely, William Justin Harsha's *Ploughed Under: The Story of an Indian Chief, Told By Himself* and Winnemucca's *Life Among the Piutes: Their Wrongs and Claims* "are narrated by strong Native American voices that address a white audience, accept the complexity of their identities, and give full accounts of their alternative histories." I have not read these books, but I gleaned much from Ben's discussion of them as vehicles for addressing the "Indian question." I was interested to learn that the main characters of Harte's and Miller's works were "mixed race" or "half-blood," a motif that inhabits much Native American fiction from the twentieth century and beyond, including works by Oliver La Farge.

The fifth book that Ben examines in "Silenced Voices, Forgotten Histories, and the Indian Question" is Helen Hunt Jackson's novel *Ramona*, which he calls "one of the country's most popular and durable texts." The title character is a "half-blood," and the novel depicts the romance between Ramona, who is unaware of her lineage, and the Indian, Alessandro.

Helen Hunt Jackson occupies a curious place in our national literary landscape. Born in 1830, she grew up in Amherst, Massachusetts where she was a childhood acquaintance of Emily Dickinson. In fact, Jackson's 1876 novel *Mercy Philbrick's Choice*, the story of a reclusive New England poet, seems to have been inspired by Dickinson. Helen's parents died when she was a teenager and her first husband, army captain Edward Hunt, was killed in New York Harbor while testing a torpedo of his own invention. The couple had lost their first son to a brain tumor, and the second boy died of diphtheria eighteen months after his father's death. Helen moved to Newport, Rhode Island, where she was encouraged to write by Dickinson's editor, Thomas Wentworth Higginson, who was also a friend to Louisa May Alcott and, as we have seen, John La Farge.When she contracted tuberculosis, Helen moved to Colorado for her health, and there she met and married banker and railroad executive, William Jackson. In Colorado, she heard a 1879 lecture by Chief Standing Bear on the abuses suffered by the Ponca Indians. Her sympathies aroused, Jackson became an advocate for Native Americans mistreated by the federal government. In 1881, she published at her own expense the pamphlet *A Century of Dishonor*, which she sent to every member of Congress. Written on the red cover of the book was "Look upon your hands: they are stained with the blood of your relations."

Jackson then traveled to California to learn about Native Americans who had been displaced from their land when California became a state. She spearheaded an investigation into these abuses, and to no avail, she encouraged the federal government to help Native Americans by setting aside land for reservations and providing other assistance. Jackson used the information from her investigation as the setting for *Ramona*. She hoped the book would influence change in the treatment of Indians in much the same way as *Uncle Tom's Cabin*, written by her lifelong friend, Harriet Beecher Stowe, had influenced people's attitudes towards slavery. While *Ramona* did become a bestseller, most readers seemed less interested in the troubles of Native Americans than they did in the ill-fated romance between Ramona and Alessandro. (This reception reminds me of the public's reaction to Oliver La Farge's second novel, *Sparks Fly Upward*. In that book, the failed love affair between Esteban and Favia was likely more compelling to the general reader than than the abuses suffered by indigenous peoples.) Helen Jackson said of her book, "I did not write *Ramona*; it was written through me. My life-blood went into it—all I had thought, felt, and suffered for five years on the Indian question."

Ramona is a deeply affecting novel full of lyrical prose in its fully realized and diverse cast of characters, and in its depiction of life on Señor Moreno's ranch, and of the love and grace in the Franciscan missions. Alessandro's descent into madness is gut-wrenching, and it's hard not to be upset by the capricious and duplicitous whites who, in defense of their own economic stronghold, blatantly disregard the rights of California's Native Americans.

A few years ago, Ben suggested I read Leslie Marmon Silko's novel *Ceremony*, a book Sherman Alexie calls "the greatest novel in Native American literature." In fact, Alexie asserts, "It is one of the greatest novels of any time and place. I have read the book so many times that I probably have it memorized. I teach it and I learn from it and I am continually in awe of its power, beauty, rage, vision, and violence." Originally published in 1977, Silko's preface to the 2006 edition details the process of writing the book while in Ketchikan, Alaska, where her husband was then working in a legal services office. Silko describes how "the novel was my refuge, my magic vehicle back to the Southwest land of sandstone mesas, blue sky, and sun."

Ceremony is the story of Tayo, a Native American veteran of World War II who returns to his home a shell of his former self, and whose healing is dependent on his tribe's stories and ceremonies. These stories, writes Larry McMurtry in the introduction, "help the people move from an imbalance and disorder back to a kind of balance, the balance that comes from the accuracy and depth and beauty of the stories." When discussing her motivation for *Ceremony*, Leslie Marmon Silko writes,

> I realized I wanted to better understand what happened to the war veterans, many of whom were survivors of the Bataan Death March, cousins and relatives of mine who returned from the war and stayed drunk the rest of their lives. [Like Ira Hayes, perhaps?] The war veterans weren't always drunk, and they were home and available to us children when the other adults were busy at work. The men were kind to us children; they helped me train with my first horse. Even as a child I knew they were not bad people, yet something had happened to them. What was it?

As the novel opens, Tayo has recently arrived at his grandmother's home in the Laguno Pueblo via a veterans' hospital. He lies in bed in a disoriented state reliving his combat experiences in the South Pacific. He recalls how "The sergeant had called for a medic and somebody rolled up [Tayo's] sleeve; they told him to sleep, and the next day they all acted as though nothing had happened. They call it battle fatigue, and they said hallucinations were common with malarial fever."

Back home, Tayo is confused and mourning for the loss of Rocky, his cousin with whom he served and who died in combat. Growing up, Rocky had been the bright star of the family, a good student and athlete with plans for the future. Now he is dead, but Tayo considers, "It was him, Tayo, who had died, but somehow there had been a mistake with the corpses, and somehow his was still unburied."

Silko's portrayal of Tayo's post-traumatic stress syndrome is incredibly visceral. Throughout the book, we see Tayo struggling with alcohol and the absence of personal identity:

> He had heard Auntie talk about the veterans—drunk all the time, she said. But he knew why. It was something the old people could not understand. Liquor was medicine for the anger that made them hurt, for the pain of the loss, medicine for tight bellies and choked-up throats. He was beginning to feel a comfortable place inside himself, close to his own beating heart, near his own warm belly; he crawled inside and watched the storm swirling on the outside and he was safe there; the winds of rage could not touch him.

During the course of *Ceremony*, Silko, through Tayo, touches on many of the the same themes found in the fiction of Oliver La Farge. For example, as evidenced above, there are the deleterious effects of alcohol. Silko also describes the pressures of assimilation and the pernicious loss of Indian identity in boarding schools and at the hands of Christian missionaries. As she writes, "Christianity separated the people from themselves; it tried to crush the single clan name, encouraging each person to stand alone, because Jesus Christ would save only the individual soul. Jesus Christ was not like the Mother who loved and cared for them as her children, as her family."

As Tayo pursues a path of personal redemption, his animosity for white people pervades his very being: "He ... hated them. Not for what they wanted to do with him, but for what they did to the earth with their machines, and the animals with their packs of dogs and their guns." Tayo calls these people "the destroyers: they work to see how much can be lost, how much can be forgotten. They destroy the feeling people have for each other." By returning to the old ceremonies, the old stories, however, Tayo is restored to himself and he makes sense of his own narrative:

> He cried the relief he felt at finally seeing the pattern, the way all the stories fit together—the old stories, the war stories—to become the story that was still being told. He was not crazy; he had never been crazy. He had only seen and heard the world as it always was: no boundaries, only transitions through all distances and time.

In his 2017 book *History and Hope in American Literature: Models of Critical Patriotism*, Ben Railton devotes a chapter to an examination of Leslie Marmon Silko's *Ceremony* and Louise Erdrich's *Love Medicine*. According to Ben,

> Both books focus for most of their lengths on the darkest of those histories and realities, bringing their young protagonists to the brink of despair and destruction as a result. Yet in both books those protagonists, armed with the best of what they have learned from their histories and communities and with their own strength and determination, instead reach powerfully hopeful epiphanies and make optimistic concluding choices, embodying in the process the hard-won hope that a fuller engagement with the extended and ongoing histories of Native Americans can offer all Americans.

Ben first considers *Ceremony* and comments on Silko's choice to make Tayo a veteran of World War II, a choice that "immediately grounds her novel in a largely forgotten yet profoundly telling and traumatic contemporary Native American history." He goes on to point out that 44,000 Native Americans, twelve percent of the Native American population at the time, served in this conflict, as contrasted with eight percent of the overall U.S. population. Ben delineates the physical and psychological symptoms of PTSD that Tayo experiences in the novel. He shows how Silko highlights the efforts to erase Native American identity. Chief among these efforts are the Indian boarding schools where traditional Native American practices and habits are forbidden. Ben touches upon the novel's depiction of assimilation, and how the Christian missionaries of the story deny expressions of Native American heritage and culture. He also mentions the endemic poverty that threatens the novel's characters, such as Tayo's mother, who is forced to become a prostitute. (As we have seen, the motifs of identity, assimilation, poverty, and prostitution also infuse the works of Oliver La Farge.) Through the traditional voices and histories he experiences, however, Tayo "ends the story on his own terms."

In his examination of *Love Medicine*, Ben considers the military service of Henry Lamartine Jr. who also experiences detrimental changes to his psyche. Ben concludes that Erdrich's "representation of military service and its destructive effects on both individuals and communities exemplifies how fully [Erdrich's] approach complements and amplifies Silko's." Ben discusses in detail the pervasive influence of alcohol in *Love Medicine*, and he notes that alcoholism links the community of the novel during the fifty years of the narrative's span. (In an interesting aside on alcohol, one of the characters in *Love Medicine* suggests that Ira Hayes's bourbon of choice was Old Grand Dad.) Erdrich's use of multiple narrators, Ben says, allows her to depict more fully than Silko the histories of women within their tribal communities; more than half of the chapters of *Love Medicine* are narrated by women, and these chapters point out the "difficulty of creating and sustaining homes and families within the reservation world." Finally, Ben writes, "Because Erdrich brings her novel and characters up to the 1980s, compared to Silko's post-World War II setting, she is also able to engage with particularly contemporary issues, ways in which dark Native American histories and identities have evolved into the late twentieth-century present." These contemporary issues include capitalizing on Native American culture and heritage for consumer entertainment and profit, as, for example, Lyman Lamartine's manufacture of rubber tomahawks.

These same contemporary issues occupy the works of Sherman Alexie, one of the most widely read of today's Native American writers. Alexie, of Spokane-Coeur d'Alene tribal ancestry, is a novelist, short story writer, poet, and filmmaker who grew up on the Spokane Indian Reservation in Washington. His first novel, *Reservation Blues*, won the American Book

Award upon its publication in 1996. The story follows several characters who grew up together on the Spokane Indian Reservation and who now, in their thirties, are musicians in the band Coyote Springs. They meet blues musician Robert Johnson who, as the legend goes, sells his soul to the devil in 1931 and then allegedly fakes his own death seven years later. Alexie's voice in the novel is plainspoken but full of both humor and pathos as he weaves together lyrical, poignant stories of Native American history and current reservation life. He describes the reservation in aching detail, cataloging, for example, the items to be found at the reservation Trading Post: "Its shelves were stocked with reservation staples: Diet Pepsi, Spam, Wonder bread, and a cornucopia of various carbohydrates, none of them complex. One corner of the Trading Post was devoted to gambling machines that had become mandatory on every reservation."

He notes the violent disconnect "for those who dreamed in childhood of fishing for salmon but woke up as adults to shop at the Trading Post and stand in line for U.S.D.A. commodity food instead. They savagely, repeatedly, opened up cans of commodities and wept over the rancid meat, forced to eat what stray dogs ignored."

Alexie addresses the notion of Native American identity in *Reservation Blues*, as one of the characters declares "You ain't really Indian unless there was some point in your life that you didn't want to be." Yet Alexie writes of how Indians, even as strangers, greet each other in familiar, intimate terms: "Every Indian is a potential lover, friend, or relative dancing over the horizon, only a little beyond it. Indians need each other that much; they need to be that close, tying themselves to each other and closing their eyes against the storm." These storms include the shared, palpable past. As one character explains to another:

> We were both at Wounded Knee when the Ghost Dancers were slaughtered. We were slaughtered at Wounded Knee. I know there were whole different tribes there, no Spokanes or Flatheads, but we were still somehow there. There was a part of every Indian bleeding in the snow. All those soldiers killed us in the name of God, enit? They shouted "Jesus Christ" as they ran swords through our bellies.

Can you feel the pain still, late at night, when you're trying to sleep, when you're praying to a God whose name was used to justify the slaughter?

Alexie reiterates these themes of identity and family in his 2007 young adult novel, *The Absolutely True Diary of a Part-Time Indian*, which won the National Book Award for Young People's Literature. Despite this recognition, the American Library Association states that Alexie's semi-autobiographical novel consistently tops the list of the most challenged or banned books in the country—a designation, Alexie says, "that makes me giddy with joy." His reaction is distinctly different from one Oliver La Farge offers when he learns that *Laughing Boy* has been banned in public school districts in Texas and Georgia. In a column in the *Santa Fe New Mexican*, La Farge laments

> Now that work, that product of mine, in a real sense my unexpectedly successful child, has been smirched. It is a false smirching. It has no real meaning. Still, it has caused me a disagreeable sensation. I feel as if some nasty person had come up to me and drawn a slimy, unwashed finger across my hand. It is his dirt, not mine, but I would sooner not have been touched.

The Absolute True Diary of a Part-Time Indian is the story of fourteen-year-old Arnold Spirit, Jr., who is desperate to escape the poverty on his Spokane Indian Reservation. As Junior says, "It sucks to be poor, and it sucks to feel that you somehow *deserve* to be poor." Being an Indian, Junior knows, means that you are somehow "destined to be poor," and he concludes, "Poverty doesn't give you strength or teach you lessons about perseverance. No, poverty only teaches you how to be poor."

Mr. P, a sympathetic white teacher at Junior's school, encourages him to attend an all-white public high school off the reservation. As Mr. P says, "If you stay on this rez, they're going to kill you. I'm going to kill you. We're all going to kill you. You can't fight us forever." Junior enrolls at Reardan High School, twenty-two miles from his home. The high school mascot is an Indian which according to Junior "[makes] me the only *other* Indian in town."

Despite resentment from people on the reservation ("They call me an apple because they think I'm red on the outside and white on the inside."), Junior's desire for a better life is supported by his provincial family and their close-knit nature. As Junior says,

> Indian families stick together like Gorilla Glue, the strongest adhesive in the world. My mother and father both lived within two miles of where they were born, and my grandmother lived one mile from where she was born. Ever since the Spokane Indian Reservation was founded back in 1881, nobody in my family had ever lived anywhere else. We Spirits stay in one place. We are absolutely tribal. For good or bad, we don't leave one another.

During the course of his year at Reardan High School, Junior makes new friends and plays on the varsity basketball team. However, he also experiences the loss of family and old friends, primarily due to the influence of alcohol. At one point, Junior describes how one of his friends, Gordy,

> gave me this book by a Russian dude named Tolstoy, who wrote: "Happy families are all alike; every unhappy family is unhappy in its own way." Well, I hate to argue with a Russian genius, but Tolstoy didn't know Indians. And he didn't know that all Indian families are unhappy for the same exact reason: the fricking booze.

Junior mourns for the members of his tribe who are dying because of their addiction to alcohol. As he concludes, "I wanted them to get strong and get sober and get the hell off the rez."

Eric Gansworth's young adult novel *If I Ever Get Out of Here: A Novel with Paintings*, published by Scholastic Press in 2013, also addresses themes of Native American dislocation and the loss of identity. The novel is the story of Lewis "Shoe" Blake, a middle schooler growing up on the Tuscarora Indian Reservation in New York in 1975. Shoe and his family are exceedingly poor, which causes him anguish when he befriends George Haddonfield, the son of an Air Force officer whose family recently moved to a nearby town.

One prevailing motif of this novel is the legacy of Indian boarding schools. Lewis remarks on the irony of being rewarded for learning the Tuscarora language in elementary school when his grandparents, survivors of Indian boarding schools, were punished for speaking in their native tongues. He tells how government agents convinced his great-grandparents to send their children away when they were young so they could learn to navigate the white world. As Shoe notes, "The United States government had sponsored these schools, where the official motto was 'Kill the Indian but save the man.' The idea was that if Indian kids were taken from their families for long enough and exposed to a different world, they'd forget their language, families, and reservation life." As Shoe later concludes, "All Indian parents had the specter of the boarding schools—the beatings, the isolation, the rape. It was a seventy-five-year-old ghost, but still one potent enough for me to listen."

Gansworth paints a dreary portrait of reservation life, and of the poverty that Shoe accepts but is tortured by nonetheless. The novel also wrestles with the notion of identity and how one's "Indianness" dictates reservation life. As Shoe relates,

> The expectations were different on the rez. There were heavy costs for marrying non-Indians, and it was worse for guys than women. If my sister had married a white man, her kids would still have legal status as Indians, but if I married a white woman, my kids would not. How could anyone make that choice, knowing what their kids' lives would be like on the reservation? They'd be treated differently, have to go to a different school, ride a different bus, and for the rest of their lives—even if they attended community events, learned how to social dance, learned the songs—everyone would know their business, and that it was different business. It was the craziest system, but it was the truth as we were bound to it.

Louise Erdrich speaks to this conundrum of identity in her novel *The Round House*, recipient of the 2012 National Book Award for Fiction. Early in the story, the narrator, Joe, describes the difficulty of ascertaining if one is indeed an Indian:

You can't tell if a person is an Indian from a set of fingerprints. You can't even tell from a local police report. You can't tell from a picture. From a mug shot. From a phone number. From the government's point of view, the only way you can tell an Indian is to look at that person's history. There must be ancestors from way back who signed some document or were recorded as Indians by the U.S. Government, someone identified as a member of a tribe. And then after that you have to look at that person's blood quantum, how much Indian blood they've got that belongs to one tribe. In most cases, the government will call the person an Indian if their blood is one-quarter—it usually has to be from one tribe. But that tribe has also got to be federally recognized. In other words, being an Indian is in some ways a tangle of red tape.

(According to Tommy Orange, this tangle of red tape began in the Virginia Colony in 1705 with the introduction of Native blood quantum. Orange writes, "If you were at least half Native, you didn't have the same rights as white people. Blood Quantum and tribal membership qualifications have since been turned over to individual tribes to decide.")

Set on an Ojibwe reservation, *The Round House* tells the story of thirteen-year-old Joe, who is frustrated by the lack of progress in the investigation of a brutal attack suffered by his mother. His mother is raped during this assault, and her son enlists his best friends to find her attacker. The novel follows Joe and his friends as they piece together clues to the crime and eventually manage to exact their revenge.

The Round House delves into the ambiguities of tribal politics and the inherent difficulty of investigating cases that involve tribal, local, and state law enforcement agencies. Accounts of violence and rape imbue the novel, and in its afterword Erdrich notes the prevalence of rape of Native American women. Quoting a 2009 report by Amnesty International, Erdrich writes, "One in three Native women will be raped in her lifetime (and that figure is certainly higher as Native women often do not report rape); 86 percent of rapes and sexual assaults upon Native women are perpetrated by non-Native men; few are prosecuted."

Sherman Alexie addresses the legacy of rape in his 2017 memoir, *You Don't Have to Say You Love Me.* The book primarily explores the complex relationship between Alexie and his mother, Lillian, who "was conceived by rape and bore a daughter as a result of rape." Alexie writes that "Rape was common on my reservation. But it was rarely discussed. And even more rarely prosecuted." He attributes this injustice to the repressive cultural strictures that protect Native men of status and power. He also notes that rape knows no gender boundaries as he describes how "Twenty years ago, I sat in a room with fifty indigenous men from all over North America as they, one by one, stood and testified about being raped by white priests, white teachers, white coaches, and white security guards and soldiers. These rapes happened in residential boarding schools all across the United States and Canada. And they happened from the late nineteenth century into the late twentieth." As Alexie concludes,

> Rape is
> Our ancestor.
> Rape is
> Our creator.
> Rape is
> Our Book
> Of Genesis.
> Rape is
> Our Adam & Eve.

Alexie explores other themes in his memoir including reservation life, assimilation, and Native identity. He describes how as a young man he'd "been trying to escape the rez for years. After all, Indian reservations were created by white men to serve as rural concentration camps, and I think that's still their primary purpose." He tells how being friends with white people means he must live in their "white world." They, on the other hand, spend little time in his "indigenous world." As he writes, being American means being white. However, Alexie points out the difficulty of assimilation because "in the Indian world, 'white' is our enemy. 'White' is the conqueror. 'White' is the liar, killer, and rapist. So if one Indian wants to inflict a grievous emotional wound on another Indian, then 'white' is the Big Fucking Gun of insults."

So, what does it mean to be Indian and how is "Indianness" gauged? Alexie addresses this question in the following way:

> The concept of "Indianness" is amorphous and highly personal and eccentric. It's hard to say what "Indianness" is without reverting to generic notions of "cultural construction" and "postcolonialism." But I will say that I have never been a dancer or a singer. I have only intermittently believed in God. I used to be a math prodigy and now I'm a great storyteller. Does any of that make me more or less Indian? I don't think so. You know what makes me and my stories Indian? *All the goddamn funerals.*

In his 2018 novel *There There*, the story of twelve disparate Native American characters who converge at the annual Big Oakland Powwow, Tommy Orange recasts the Native American notion of identity and belonging. In a *New Yorker Radio Hour* podcast from July of 2018, Orange discusses his background, his motivation for writing the book, and the novel's format. Orange admits to possessing little intellectual curiosity growing up, but says that changed when he read John Kennedy O'Toole's *The Confederacy of Dunces*, which showed him what a novel "could do."

Orange started to write, and his writing took on more form as he incorporated elements of his own experience into his fiction. He decided to attend the Institute of Native American Arts in Santa Fe (where he now teaches), and was emboldened by the community of writers there, who understood him and his context without his having to explain. He realized that there are few, if any, novels about urban Native Americans, perhaps because their experiences are considered less authentic than the experiences of reservation-based Indians. With *There There*, he wanted to capture the polyphonic voices of urban Native Americans, and thereby challenge the monolithic view of Native American culture.

The prologue to *There There* describes how white society traditionally defined and continues to "slander" Native American life and culture. The list of these offenses include "Kevin Costner saving us, John Wayne's six-shooter slaying us, an Italian guy named Iron Eyes Cody playing our parts in movies … We have all the logos and mascots … Our heads are on flags, jerseys, and coins."

Orange writes that the migration of Native Americans to cities, fueled by economic necessity, was meant to be the final step of assimilation into American culture, "the completion of a five-hundred-year-old genocidal campaign." However, Orange asserts, "the city made us new, and we made it ours." Orange characterizes Urban Indians as "the generation born in the city. We've been moving for a long time, but the land moves with you like memory. An Urban Indian belongs to the city, and cities belong to the earth … Being Indian has never been about returning to the land. The land is everywhere or nowhere."

The Urban Indian protagonists of *There There* possess distinct voices and distinct identities, yet collectively, Orange suggests, they reflect the lives of contemporary Native American city dwellers. One adult narrator suffers from the "Drome," or fetal alcohol syndrome. Another is a veteran of the 1969 siege of Alcatraz. Another speaker is addicted to the internet, and still another works as a suicide prevention counselor for Native American communities. Other narrators seek to understand what it means to be an Indian through immersion in tradition or by wrestling with ancestral ghosts.

In the novel's "Interlude," Orange explains that "We made powwows because we needed a place to be together. Something intertribal, something old, something to make us money, something we could work toward, for our jewelry, our songs, our dances, our drum." The characters of this novel, for these and other reasons, travel to the Big Oakland Powwow and once there experience a powerful and unexpected event. Again in the "Interlude" (and in his own voice), Orange comments on what it means to be a Native American:

When we go to tell our stories, people think we want it to have gone different. People want to say things like "sore losers" and "move on already," "quit playing the blame game." But is it a game? Only those who have lost as much as we have see the particularly nasty slice of smile on someone who thinks they're winning when they say

"Get over it." This is the thing: If you have the option to not think about or even consider history, whether you learned it right or not, whether it even deserves consideration, that's how you know you're on board the ship that serves hors d'oeuvres and fluffs your pillows, while others are out at sea, swimming or drowning, or clinging to little inflatable rafts that they take turns keeping inflated, people short of breath, who've never even heard the words *hors d'oeuvres* or *fluff*.

⋘⋙

The works I've discussed above are just an appetizer, the hors d'oeuvres if you will, of the rich feast of Native American literature. While they are immensely satisfying, I'm eager to taste more, to consume or at least sample, the varied entries on the literature menu. I also certainly need to read more nonfiction to enhance my palate, perhaps beginning with *Everything You Know About Indians Is Wrong* by Paul Chant Smith and *The Inconvenient Indian* by Thomas King. According to Tommy Orange, "If you feel as if you don't know anything, or that what you know might be wrong—whether you're native or not—these two books are either a great place to start or a great place to start reassessing what you think you might know." So it appears that my education must continue.

ACKNOWLEDGEMENTS

I am indebted to many people for the support and encouragement they gave me during the writing of this book. Thanks to Michael Hemenway who helped me think through the structure of the narrative. I'm grateful to Paul Erb who invited me to talk about Oliver La Farge with his American literature students at Woodberry Forest School. Janine St. Germain graciously sent me facsimiles of archived editions of *The Budget* from Saint Bernard's School, and Peter Brooks shed light on student life at Saint Bernard's, Groton, and Harvard. In New Orleans, Dr. Hortensio Calvo entertained my inquiries at Tulane University's Latin American Library, and Eric Seifort provided access to La Farge related materials at the Historic New Orleans Collection. Thanks also to Ben Railton for his friendship and scholarship.

I am appreciative of the work of LaFarge biographers Robert A. Hecht, T. M. Pearce, and especially D'Arcy McNickle. Their books informed and influenced my investigation of the life of Oliver La Farge. Many thanks to Ken Wilson for his copyediting expertise and to CJ Green for his thoughts regarding publication. I owe a huge thank you to Laura Roseberry for her editing and design talents. Thank you, Laura.

The encouragement and suggestions of my first readers spurred me to complete my manuscript. Thank you to these readers: my siblings, Buck, Alison, and Lucy; my friend Paul Walker; and, of course, my wife, Susie.

Finally, many thanks and much love to my daughter, Elise, who patiently escorted her parents to La Farge sites in New York City, and to Susie, who welcomed Oliver La Farge into our home these last three years.

SOURCES OF QUOTATIONS

PREFACE

5 "Zing! Zup! Zing! Zup!": Dingledine, Raymond C., Lena Barksdale and Marion Belt Nesbit. *Virginia's History*, 26–27.

6 "wanted to tell a new generation": Springston, Rex. *Happy Slaves? The peculiar story of three Virginia school textbooks.* (*Richmond Times Dispatch*, 4/18/18).

7 "To explode the Pocahontas legend": *ibid.*

7 "more romance than history": *ibid.*

7 "a feeling of strong affection": Simkins, Francis Butler, Spotswood Hunnicut Jones and Sidman P. Poole. *Virginia: History, Government, Geography*, 369.

7 "stepped proudly, as if he knew": Springston, Rex. *Happy Slaves?*

7 "did not work so hard": *ibid.*

7 "Thomas Nelson Page says": Willis, Saunders. *The Story of Virginia*, 263.

8 "The little white boys": *ibid*, 262.

8 "always near the little girls"; "had their own little maids": *ibid*, 263.

8 "every heart in the South": *ibid*, 318.

9 "William Faulkner was asked": Gwynn, Frederick and Joseph Blotner, eds. *Faulkner in the University: Class Conferences at the University of Virginia*, 13–14.

9 "a better life for both": Springston, Rex. *Happy Slaves?* (*Richmond Times Dispatch*, 4/18/18)

9 "War was the only method": *ibid*, 31.

9 "We must not forget"; "capable of being": *ibid*, 32.

9 "mode of living": Sydenstricker, Edgar and A. I. Burger. *School History of Virginia*, 15.

9 "Almost everybody in our state": Smith, E. Erlich. *Our Virginia: A Description of Virginia for Young People*, Preface.

10 "Indians did not want": *ibid*, 3.

10 "The Indian's future": Hemphill, William Edwin, Marvin Wilson Schlagel and Sadie Ethel Engelberg. *Cavalier Commonwealth: History and Government of Virginia*, 18.

10 "had trouble with the Indians": Willis, Saunders. *The Story of Virginia*, 14.

10 "He looked up and saw": *ibid*, 38.

11 "Among the poets": Wayland, John. *A History of Virginia for Boys and Girls*, 26.

12 "renounced publicly": Kupperman, Karen Ordahl. *Pocahontas and the English Boys: Caught Between Cultures in Early Virginia*, 98.

12 "bear the image"; what were we before": *ibid*, 85. Much of the information about Pocahontas found here comes from Kupperman's book.

13 "Today in Virginia": Dingledine, Barksdale, Nesbit. *Virginia's History*, 48.

13 "all that refined taste" et al: Family document.

13 "If the Virginia General Assembly": *Charlottesville Daily Progress*, 10/22/18.

14 "In mocking Warren": *ibid*.

14 "these children were held": Bell, Edith Rathbun and William Lightfoot Heartwell, Jr.: *Brunswick Story: A History of Brunswick County*, 21.

15 "Nearly every section": *Hand Book Brunswick County, Virginia*, 13.

15 "This statue in Charlottesville"; "I can say for myself": *Charlottesville Daily Progress*, 11/15/2019.

16 "Don't let the name": www.wikipedia.com

16 "murderin' half-breed": Clemens, S. L. *The Adventures of Tom Sawyer*, 60.

16 "the wretchedest type": Twain, Mark. *Roughing It*, 131–132.

16 "Few white people understand": Harvey, Robert A. *Oliver La Farge as a Literary Interpreter of Navajo Indian Culture*, 42.

17 Today writer Tommy Orange: *The Washington Post*, 11/21/18.

17 "transcription but ... an attempt": Hampl, Patricia. *The Art of the Wasted Day*, 124–125.

18 "Dr. Whitney Azoy": www.mei.edu.

18 "is not only the first"; "entails the aggressive struggle": www.amazon.com.

19 "study of paradoxes": Pearce, T. M. *Oliver La Farge*, Preface.

19 "position ... in modern American fiction": Kleinpoppen, Paul. "Some Notes on Oliver La Farge", 70.

19 "I almost never travel": Hampl. *The Art of the Wasted Day*, 46.

19 "pilgrimages ... to the homes": *ibid*, 44.

PART I: NEW ENGLAND

21 "at the helm of *Windingo*": La Farge, Oliver. Raw Material, 26.

21 "was most anxious to avoid"; "she hated a stuck-up boy": ibid, 24.

22 "is one of the most": www.nndb.com.

22 "an artist of broad": www.phillipscollection.org.

23 "forefront of the American": www.americanart.si.edu.

23 "exotic subjects, spontaneous brush work": www.phillipscollection.org.

23 "exercised a considerable personal": www.americanart.si.edu.

26 "moved in before the plaster": Yarnell, James L. *John La Farge: A Biographical and Critical Study*, 43.

28 "is dedicated to a different": Excerpted from informational brochure for The Cathedral Church of Saint John the Divine.

28 "In the angel idea": *The Literary Digest*, Vol. XXXI, No. 17 (October 21, 1905).

30 "The national Delta Psi": Dew, Charles B. *The Making of a Racist*, 78–79.

31 "old Delta Psi house": Blotner, Joseph. *Faulkner: A Biography*, 277.

32 "A boy might be": La Farge, Oliver. *Raw Material*, 37.

33 "He had given me": *ibid*, 151.

33 "In this book": Parsons, Elsie Crews, ed. *American Indian Life*, 2.

34 "Center, the stone ring": *ibid*, 418.

34 "do their share"; "from ambassadors to the": Pearce, T. M. *Oliver La Farge*, 25.

35 All quotations from *The Budget* are taken from facsimiles sent to me by Janine St. Germain of St. Bernard's School

38 "At Groton it was important": La Farge, Oliver. *Raw Material*, 9.

39 "One needed to be:" *ibid*, 12.

40 "was my release and great": *ibid*, 47.

41 "There is something wrong": McNickle, D'Arcy. *Indian Man: A Life of Oliver La Farge*, 25.

41 "Rowing at School": La Farge, Oliver. *Raw Material*, 67.

41 "which is, with six": McNickle, D'Arcy. *Indian Man*, 24.

41 "You have known complete": La Farge, Oliver. *Raw Material*, 71.

42 "a howling ash-heap": Caffey, David L., ed. *Yellow Sun, Bright Sky: The Indian Country Stories of Oliver La Farge*, 1.

42 "The Indians had got me": *ibid*, 2.

42 "The men of the Old": La Farge, *Raw Material*, 153.

45 All quotations from *Southern Workman* and *Hampton School Record* are taken from the following source: https://catalog.hathitrust.org/Record/000642422

46 All quotations from *"A Trip Made in Behalf of the Indian Rights Association to Some Indian Reservations of the Southwest* by S. C. Armstrong are taken from the following source: https://babel.hathitrust.org/cgi/pt?id=mdp.39015026613821&view =1up&seq=9

PART II: NEW ORLEANS

49 "In March, 1924": Blom, Frans and Oliver La Farge. *Tribes and Temples*, 1.

50 "the sections on archaeology": *ibid*, 1.

50 "Lazaro Hernandez Guillermo": *ibid*, 450.

51 "It is our hope": *ibid*, 449.

51 "is somewhat of a weak sister": Reed, John Shelton. *Dixie Bohemia: A French Quarter Circle in the 1920s*, 130.

52 "Up early and into": La Farge, Oliver. *Journal of First Tulane Expedition, 1925*, no page given.

53 "It is in Guatemala": Grandin, Levenson, Oglesby. *The Guatemala Reader: History, Culture, Politics*, 185.

53 "what a boon this is": *ibid*.

53 "Off at 9:30": La Farge, Oliver. *Journal of First Tulane Expedition, 1925*, no page given.

54 "April 15th, Villa Hermosa": *ibid*.

54 "Today, decoration day": *ibid*.

54 "All Guatemalan officials": *ibid*.

55 "a sort of Creole version": Reed, John Shelton. *Dixie Bohemia*, 13.

55 "a decaying monument": *ibid*, 16.

55 "My mother told me": La Farge, Oliver. *Raw Material*, 114–115.

56 "a place in which": Reed, John Shelton. *Dixie Bohemia*, 131.

56 "I was discovering": La Farge, Oliver. *Raw Material*, 112–113.

56 "a slatternly washerwoman": Reed, John Shelton. *Dixie Bohemia*, 61.

57 "his tabletop mock-Indian Eagle Dance": Reed, John Shelton. *Dixie Bohemia*, 16.

57 "a bottle of absinthe": *ibid*, 22.

57 "largely conducted at open windows": *ibid*, 74.

57 "*Mosquitoes* was a jumping-off place": Karl, Frederick in the Introduction to *Mosquitoes* by William Faulkner, xi.

57 "resembling a benevolent walrus": Faulkner, William. *Mosquitoes*, 31.

57 "I got a job": *ibid*, 121.

58 "I got to talking": *ibid*, 149–150.

58 "Outside the window": *ibid*, 7.

58 "a sort of private joke": Reed, John Shelton. *Dixie Bohemia*, 1.

59 "the first fifty decorated": Spratling, William and William Faulkner. *Sherwood Anderson and Other Famous Creoles: A Gallery of Contemporary New Orleans*, viewed at the Historic New Orleans Collection, April 2019.

59 "forty people ... spend day after day": *ibid*.

59 "trouble with us American artists": *ibid*.

60 "flaunt my opinions or": Reed, John Shelton. *Dixie Bohemia*, 61.

61 "The Department of Middle American Research": Tulane University, *Jambalaya*, 1927.

61 "was not like most": La Farge, Oliver. *All the Young Men*, 66.

61 "You will ask for one": La Farge, Oliver, *ibid*, 77.

62 "chose small, nucleated settlements": Grandin, Levenson, Oglesby. *The Guatemala Reader*, 187.

62 "rely heavily on key informants": *ibid*, 186.

62 "Few people realize the task": La Farge, Oliver and Douglas Byers. *The Year Bearer's People*, no page given.

63 "the survival of old beliefs": La Farge, Oliver and Douglas Byers. *ibid*, 8.

63 "to present the ethnology": *ibid*, 8.

63 "possessed important secret information": *ibid*, 23.

63 "such an informant as one": *ibid*, 33.

64 "the only way to do": La Farge, Oliver. *Raw Material*, 85.

64 "I've started a novel": McNickle, D'Arcy. *Indian Man*, 45.

65 "Dramatic early dislocations": Lee, Hermione. *Willa Cather: Double Lives*, 30.

65 "It was while crossing": McNickle, D'Arcy. *Indian Man*, 55.

65 "Laughing Boy expressed the point": La Farge, Oliver, *Raw Material*, 177.

65 "soaked in Indian literature": *ibid*, 204.

66 "in this book I should": *ibid*, 205.

66 "I have been as accurate": La Farge, Oliver. *Laughing Boy*, introduction (1929 edition).

66 "This book was written": La Farge, Oliver. *Laughing Boy*, Foreward (1962 edition).

66 "[The Navajo] are an unhappy people": *ibid*.

67 "would have completely staggered": *ibid*.

67 "That leaves the gratification": *ibid*.

67 "his insides all were *hozoji*": La Farge, Oliver. *Laughing Boy*, 2 (1929 edition). All quotes from the novel will be subsequently referred to by page numbers of this text.

70 "brought outlandish subject matter": McNickle, D'Arcy. *Indian Man*, 55.

70 "the key to [La Farge's] success": Kleinpoppen, Paul. "Some Notes on Oliver Lafarge", 72.

71 "turns utilitarian motions": Harvey, Robert A. "Oliver La Farge as a Literary Interpreter of Navajo Indian Culture."

71 "I don't give a damn": Pearce, T. M. *Oliver La Farge*, 112.

72 "I do not recall": Brokaw, Zoanne Sherlock. Oliver La Farge: His Fictional Navajo", 1.

72 "To the People": Harvey, Robert A. "Oliver La Farge as a Literary Interpreter of Navajo Indian Culture", 77.

73 "An almost perfect specimen": *ibid*, 13.

73 "a novel of Indian life": *ibid*, 13.

73 "is one of the most": *ibid*, 13.

73 "[It] is at every point": *ibid*, 13.

73 "*Laughing Boy* has stood out": *ibid*, 13.

73 "A comment from the back cover" *et al*: www.librarything.com.

76 "No writer can form": La Farge, Oliver. *Raw Material*, 206.

76 All quotations from the playbill of *Laughing Boy* come from the 1931–1932 yearbook of Le Petit Theatre Du Vieux Carre.

79 Transcription of the trailer for *Laughing Boy* based on the clip found on YouTube.

PART III: NEW YORK

83 "[*Laughing Boy*] was the culmination": La Farge, Oliver. *Raw Material*, 124–125.

84 "I am delighted with": McNickle, D'Arcy. *Indian Man*, 94.

84 "the tricky rhythm tapped": *ibid*, 69

85 "As I detached myself": La Farge, Oliver. *Raw Material*, 196.

85 "all Indian policy was": McNickle, D'Arcy. *Indian Man*, 71.

85 "All [government officials] were united": *ibid*, 72.

85 "Allotment is the practice": Treuer, Anton. *Everything You Wanted to Know about Indians But Were Afraid to Ask*, 91.

86 "If we look back": Treuer, David. *The Heartbeat of Wounded Knee: Native America from 1890 to the Present*, 146.

86 "Six-year-old Navajo children": Harvey, Robert A. "Oliver La Farge as a Literary Interpreter of Navajo Indian Culture", 48.

86 "return[ed] as strangers, ill-adjusted": *ibid*, 50.

86 "could not see the beauty": McNickle, D'Arcy. *Indian Man*, 74.

86 "fail to look on the Indian": *ibid*, 195.

87 "the son of Grant La Farge": La Farge, Oliver. *Sparks Fly Upward*, 1931. All quotes from the novel will be subsequently referred to by page numbers of this text.

91 "It seems to me": McNickle, D'Arcy. *Indian Man*, 100–101.

91 "In three years things settle": La Farge, Oliver. *Long Pennant*, 1933. All quotes from the novel will be subsequently referred to by page numbers of this text.

95 "These pastures were not": La Farge, Christopher. *Hoxsie Sells His Acres*, 10.

96 "a flexible instrument": Chamberlain, John. *The New York Times*, 6/15/1934.

96 "Mr. La Farge's verse": *ibid*.

96 "unlikely liking ... for a species": Hutchinson, Percy. *The New York Times*, 6/17/1934.

96 "that is ingrainedly American": *ibid*.

97 "The kindly big brother"; "he and I assumed": McNickle, D'Arcy. *Indian Man*, 58–59.

97 "A counterpoint to *Laughing Boy*": Kleinpopper, Paul. "Some Notes on Oliver La Farge", 96.

97 "The novel catalogs": McNickle, D'Arcy. *Indian Man*, 103.

98 "It is not my purpose": La Flesche, Francis. *The Middle Years: Indian Schoolboys of the Omaha Tribe*, xv–xvi.

98 "When we entered the Mission School": *ibid*, xvii.

98 "All the Indian boys": *ibid*, xvii.

98 "misconception of Indian life"; "no native American": *ibid*, xviii–xix.

98 "The white people speak": *ibid*, xx.

99 Indian children were six times": Treuer, David. *The Heartbeat of Wounded Knee*, 140.

99 "inspired and brutal benevolence": La Farge, Oliver. *A Pictorial History of the American Indian*.

100 "Call him Myron": La Farge, Oliver. *The Enemy Gods*, 1937, 7. All quotes from the novel will be subsequently referred to by page numbers of this text.

100 "'Begay' comes from the Navajo *Biye*": Preston, Douglas. *Talking to the Ground: One Family's Journey on Horseback Across the Sacred Land of the Navajo*, 276.

103 "he placed a high value": Caffey, David L., ed. *Yellow Sun, Bright Sky*, 5.

103 "Just out of school": *ibid*, 46.

104 "The face was Indian": *ibid*, 47.

104 "While we want our children"; "is all shame and fear": *ibid*, 53.

104 "nice pretty things"; "What can I do here?": *ibid*, 59.

104 "he's a bad man": *ibid*, 60.

104 "very frilly, elaborate, negligee": *ibid*, 65.

105 "As a man full of needs and wants": La Farge, Oliver. *All the Young Men*, 32.

105 "Always he saw short hair": *ibid*, 37.

105 "Slayer of the Enemy Gods": *ibid*, 43.

105 "It was a cry from the soul": McNickle, D'Arcy. *Indian Man*, 96.

PART IV: NEW MEXICO

107 "wore a smart going-away dress": La Farge, Oliver. *Behind the Mountains*, 14.

107 "a book of this kind": La Farge, Oliver. *Behind the Mountains*, v.

107 "one of the aims of this book": *ibid*, vi.

108 "simply sitting and listening": *ibid*, vii.

108 "broadly speaking … covers two villages": *ibid*, 1.

108 "looking back across an abyss": *ibid*, 5.

108 "The slippers had been bought": *ibid*, 11.

108 "Don José's idea": *ibid*, 18.

109 "Don José had seemed": *ibid*, 166.

109 "Love will not always be practical": *ibid*, 178–179.

110 "We have been expecting" Hecht, Robert A. *Oliver La Farge and the American Indian*, 136.

110 "it's way past time": *ibid*, 136.

110 "staggered by delightful reality": Scott, Winfield Townley, ed. *The Man with the Calabash Pipe: Some Observations by Oliver La Farge*, 24.

110 "harsh … insatiable land": *ibid*, 15.

110 "the people aside": La Farge, John Pen. *Turn Left at the Sleeping Dog: Scripting the Santa Fe Legend, 1920-1955*, 43.

110 "Above this screen tower": *ibid*, 44.

111 "Santa Fe has the possibility": *ibid*, 45.

111 "Because they heard": Pearce, T. M. *Oliver La Farge*, 47.

111 "warmth and rewards": Scott, Winfield Townley, ed. *The Man with the Calabash Pipe*, 8.

111 "the habit people have": Scott, Winfield Townley, ed. *The Man with the Calabash Pipe*, 10.

111 "La Farge, as much as any man": Hillerman, Tony, ed. *The Spell of New Mexico*, 1-2.

112 "live in deep poverty": *ibid*, 16.

112 "What is New Mexico, then?": *ibid*, 21.

112 "mystery and promise": La Farge, Oliver. *The Copper Pot*, 1942, 1. All quotes from the novel will be subsequently referred to by page numbers of this text.

113 "closely parallels the course": McNickle, D'Arcy. *Indian Man*, 133.

118 "Whenever our men": Balchen, Brent, Corey Ford, Oliver La Farge. *War Below Zero: The Battle for Greenland*.

118 "I'm coming more and more": McNickle, D'Arcy. *Indian Man*, 145.

119 "fresh and honest personal narrative": La Farge, Oliver. *Raw Material*, 5.

119 "record the America of one individual": *ibid*.

119 "Out of this autobiography": Engle, Paul. "Oliver La Farge Writes of His Far Travels Thru Life." Review of *Raw Material* found inside copy of book, newspaper and date not shown.

119 "All writing is in one sense": La Farge, Oliver. *Raw Material*, 2.

119 "the only reasonable answer": *ibid*, 2.

119 "the artist … is his own chief source": *ibid*, 3.

120 "fatiguing work": *ibid*, 199

120 "a life rather than an occupation": *ibid*,199

120 "Everything else will revolve": *ibid*, 200.

120 "to tell the truth"; "This enabled me": *ibid*, 203

120 "You write": *ibid*, 210.

121 "is written with grace and charm": Hecht, Robert A. *Oliver La Farge and the American Indian*, 147.

121 "general commentary on the local scene": Scott, Winfield Townley, ed. *The Man with the Calabash Pipe*.

121 "Whenever I was with him": *ibid*, xv.

121 "held opinions strongly": *ibid*, xix.

121 "could be a tough *hombre*": *ibid*, xix.

122 "Thomas Wentworth Higginson": *ibid*, xxi.

122 "the degradation of the meaning of words": *ibid*, 112.

122 "Good English, correct, standard English": *ibid*, 118.

122 "Educationists are the bunch": *ibid*, 186.

123 "[Educationists} have gone far": *ibid*, 186.

123 "is fiction based on fact": La Farge. *Cochise of Arizona (The Pipe of Peace Is Broken)*, 1955. All quotes from the novel will be subsequently referred to by page numbers of this text.

126 "This book, composed from the columns": La Farge, Oliver, with the assistance of Arthur N. Morgan. *Santa Fe: The Autobiography of a Southwestern Town*, vi.

126 "The *New Mexican* first appeared": *ibid*, xi.

126 "is to give the feel": *ibid*, xii.

126 "consisted of four pages": *ibid*, 3.

126 "The Navajoes are on their walks": *ibid*, 11–12.

127 "it is my disagreeable duty": *ibid*, 13.

127 "peaceably if possible": *ibid*, 15.

127 "to go upon a reservation": *ibid*, 54.

127 "The Navajoes are a savage and barbarous people" et al: *ibid*, 62.

127 "Surely, no Southerner": *ibid*, 63.

127 "The most important arrivals"; "every law-abiding man": *ibid*, 101.

127 "If a shell had hit": *ibid*, 104.

128 "The trouble between Garrett and Brazil": *ibid*, 193.

128 "The Most Reverend John Baptist Lamy": *ibid*, 132.

129 "Nellie Bly, the plucky young woman reporter": *ibid*, 141.

129 "Santa Fe has more advantages": *ibid*, 134.

129 "Young men, ye who dally": *ibid*, 156

129 "Miss Fertility, or Mrs."; "The Fertility panel": *ibid*, 395.

130 "That the Indians of the Southwest": *ibid*, 273.

130 "Nearly one hundred years": *ibid*, 372.

130 "Navajoes are subsisting on"; "a hope and a possibility": *ibid*, 373.

131 "New Mexico changes"; "The horses behaved admirably": *ibid*, 420.

131 "To my mother, my father, and my grandmother": La Farge, John Pendaries. *Turn Left at the Sleeping Dog: Scripting the Santa Fe Legend, 1920–1955*, Dedication.

131 "saw both a culmination"; "what many of those": *ibid*, 1.

132 "Dear Sirs:": *ibid*, 298.

132 "There are three principal social groups": *ibid*, 299.

132 "change [that] has not"; "We are no longer": *ibid*, 377.

132 "From Mexico there comes": *ibid*, 377.

132 "has become separated"; "is becoming like any other city": *ibid*, 379.

133 "Santa Fe has been": *ibid*, 379–380.

133 "the kind of writer": Pearce, T. M. *Oliver La Farge*, 85.

133 "The Navajos do not want": Harvey, Robert A. *Oliver La Farge as a Literary Interpreter of Navajo Indian Culture*, 28.

133 "feeding every stranger who passes": *ibid*, 85–86.

134 "a repository for individuals"; "For a century and a half": *ibid*, 48.

134 "The Indians were assaulted": Scott, Winfield Townley, ed. *The Man with the Calabash Pipe*, 164.

135 "One big fact stands out": La Farge, Oliver. *A Pictorial History of the American Indian*, 230.

135 "subject to federal law": *ibid*, 241.

135 "Indians do not get pensions": *ibid*, 244.

135 "until 1929 it had a general direction": *ibid*, 245–247.

135 "that no general statement": *ibid*, 248.

135 "An Indian seeking employment"; "The picture is dreary": *ibid*, 264.

136 Interview with Oliver La Farge on "Longines Chronoscope": https://www.youtube.com/watch?v=48UzUvhzXFY&list=ULqqb-u7FT7Oo&index=1898

138 "Pete wanted to just ride": Schulman, Sandra Hale. *Don't Tell Me How I Looked Falling: The Ballad of Peter La Farge*, location 445–454.

139 "he and I are inclined": Hecht, Robert A. *Oliver La Farge and the American Indian*, 241.

140 "I must say that I consider"; "Pete, I'm sure you surmised": Schulman, Sandra Hale. *Don't Tell How I Looked Falling*, location 651–696.

140 "eliminates responsibility to a community": *ibid*, location 598–602.

140 "I've finally lost the burning desire": *ibid*, location 1043.

140 "swimming in unreality": *ibid*, location 1175.

141 "Sometime around 1960": *ibid*, location 1209.

141 "hanging onto a moving car": *ibid*, location 1223.

141 "Pete is one of the unsung heroes": *ibid*. location 79–83.

141 "I was very young": *ibid*, location 1458–1462.

142 "she loved with all her heart": *ibid*, location 3017–3023.

142 "It was easy to see": Hilburn, Robert. *Johnny Cash: The Life*, 263.

143 "His voice was a voice crying": Schulman, Sandra Hale. *Don't Tell How I Looked Falling*, location 90.

143 "Peter was very proud of his heritage": Hilburn, Robert. *Johnny Cash*, 263.

143 "Look at it closely": *ibid*, 264.

143 "DJs, station managers, owners, etc.": Miller, Stephen. *Johnny Cash: The Life of an American Icon*, 123.

144 "gutless to say"; "'The Ballad of Ira Hayes' is strong medicine": *ibid*, 123.

144 "Something unusual happened": Bradley, James with Ron Powers. *Flags of Our Fathers*, 3.

145 "were about to enter a battle": *ibid*, 147.

146 "6 enlisted men and/or officers": *ibid*, 268.

146 "slapped him into something resembling sobriety": *ibid*, 290.

147 "Ira beheld the image": *ibid*, 327.

147 "On the frigid morning of January 24, 1955": *ibid*, 332.

147 *The Outsider* (Universal Studios, 1961): Directed by Delbert Mann.

149 "He is beyond us": Shulman, Sandra Hale. *Don't Tell How I Looked Falling*, location 3512–3516.

149 "book of a guy who's withdrawn": Krim, Seymour. *you & me*, 7.

149 "The last clear, definite, stamped"; "Less than six months later": *ibid*, 147.

150 "I had love for Pete La Farge": *ibid*, 149.

150 "the tall, muscular, battered body": *ibid*, 154.

150 "he wanted to be": *ibid*, 159

150 "Yet there was something fantastically": *ibid*, 148.

150 "could only plot with inspiration"; "the proud and sterile don": *ibid*, 149.

150 "the son finally admitting": *ibid*, 156.

150 "It still bewilders me": *ibid*, 157.

151 "I did not become a convert"; "What my creed finally came to be": La Farge, Oliver. *Raw Material*, 101.

152 "Oliver La Farge Is Dead at 61; Author Helped Indians Cause": *The New York Times*, 8/3/1963.

152 "Pete could hardly organize": Schulman, Sandra Hale. *"Don't Tell How I Looked Falling Down*, location 3267.

152 "Oliver La Farge is a name": *ibid*, location 3222–3246.

153 "curious": Kleinpoppen, Paul. "Some Notes on Oliver La Farge", 70.

154 "With the novels of Oliver La Farge": Harvey, Robert A. "Oliver La Farge as a Literary Interpreter of Navajo Indian Culture", 11.

154 "Into the consciousness of Americans": McNickle, D'Arcy. *Indian Man*, 236.

154 "A comparison of La Farge": "Kleinpoppen, Paul. "Some Notes on Oliver La Farge", 118.

155 "Oliver La Farge was not a great man": Hecht, Robert A. *Oliver La Farge and the American Indian*, 326.

155 "He was not a kind man": *ibid*, 330.

155 "He did have genius in him": *ibid*, 326.

155 "the fact that [La Farge] never repeated"; "His failure to grow": McNickle, D'Arcy. *Indian Man*, 20

AFTERWORD

157 "the sentiment (and it is a sentiment)": Treuer, David. *Native American Fiction: A User's Manual*, 4.

157 "My argument is not about": *ibid*, 26.

158 "When I was very young": Erdrich, Louise. *Love Medicine*, 14–15.

158 "I'd still be Marie": *ibid*, 128.

159 "A woman of detachable parts": *ibid*, 82.

159 "And so when they tell you": *ibid*, 217.

159 "The writing in this book": Orange, Tommy. "Native American Heritage Month." *Washington Post*, 11/21/2018.

160 "how the myth of the West": Railton, Ben. *Contesting the Past, Reconstructing the Nation: American Literature and Culture in the Gilded Age, 1876–1893*, 74.

161 "to narrate their histories and identities": *ibid*, 79.

161 "are narrated by strong Native American voices": *ibid*, 79.

161 "one of the country's most popular": *ibid*, 78.

162 "Look upon your hands": Griskey, Michele. *Emily Dickinson*, 79.

162 "I did not write *Ramona*": unsigned "Afterword" to Fisher Press edition of *Ramona* by Helen Hunt Jackson, 400.

163 "the greatest novel": Silko, Leslie Marmon. *Ceremony*, from the back cover.

163 "the novel was my refuge": *ibid*, from the preface.

163 "help the people move": *ibid*, xxii.

163 "I realized I wanted": *ibid*, from the preface.

163 "The sergeant had called: *ibid*, 7.

164 "It was him, Tayo": *ibid*, 25.

164 "He had heard Auntie talk": *ibid*, 37.

164 "Christianity separated the people": 62.

164 "He ... hated them": *ibid*, 189.

164 "the destroyers: they work to see how much": *ibid*, 213.

165 "He cried the relief": *ibid*, 229.

165 "Both books focus": Railton, Ben. *History and Hope in American Literature: Models of Critical Patriotism*, 29.

165 "immediately grounds her novel": *ibid*, 29.

166 "ends the story on his own terms": *ibid*, 43.

166 "representation of military service": *ibid*, 34.

166 "difficulty of creating and sustaining": *ibid*, 36–37.

166 "Because Erdrich brings her novel": *ibid*, 37.

167 "Its shelves were stocked": Alexie, Sherman. *Reservation Blues*, 12.

167 "You ain't really Indian": *ibid*, 98.

167 "Every Indian is a potential lover": *ibid*, 151.

167 "We were both at Wounded Knee": *ibid*, 167.

168 "that makes me giddy": Alexie, Sherman. *You Don't Have to Say You Love Me: A Memoir*, 339.

168 "Now that work": Scott, Winfield Townley, ed. *The Man with the Calabash Pipe*, 103.

168 "It sucks to be poor" et al: Alexie, Sherman. *The Absolute True Diary of a Part-Time Indian*, 13.

168 "If you stay on this rez": *ibid*, 43.

168 "[makes] me the only *other* Indian": *ibid*, 56.

169 "They call me an apple": *ibid*, 132.

169 "Indian families stick together": *ibid*, 89.

169 "gave me this book": *ibid*, 200.

169 "I wanted them to get": *ibid*, 216.

170 "The United States government": Gansworth, Eric. *If I Ever Get Out of Here: A Novel with Paintings*, 108.

170 "All Indian parents": *ibid*, 231.

170 "The expectations were different": *ibid*, 181.

171 "You can't tell if a person": Erdrich, Louise. *The Round House*, 29–30.

171 "If you were at least": Orange, Tommy. *There There*, 137.

171 "One in three Native women": Erdrich, Louise. *The Round House*, 319.

172 "Rape was common": "Alexie, Sherman. *You Don't Have to Say You Love Me*, 146.

172 "Twenty years ago": *ibid*, 175.

172 "Rape is": *ibid*, 408.

172 "been trying to escape": *ibid*, 200.

172 "in the Indian world": *ibid*, 427.

173 "The concept of 'Indianness'": *ibid*, 260.

174 "Kevin Costner saving us": Orange, Tommy. *There There*, 7.

174 "the completion of": *ibid*, 8.

174 "the generation born in the city": *ibid*, 11.

174 "We made powwows": *ibid*, 135.

174 "When we go to tell": *ibid* 137–138.

WORKS CITED

Alexie, Sherman. *The Absolutely True Diary of a Part-Time Indian*. New York: Little, Brown, and Company, 2007.

_____. *Reservation Blues*. New York: The Atlantic Monthly Press, 1995.

_____. *You Don't Have to Say You Love Me: A Memoir*. New York: Little, Brown, and Company, 2017.

Balchen, Berntt, Corey Ford and Oliver La Farge. *War Below Zero: The Battle for Greenland*. London: Allen & Unwin, 1945.

Bell, Edith Rathbun and William Lightfoot Heartwell, Jr. *Brunswick Story: A History of Brunswick County*. Lawrenceville, Virginia: Brunswick Times-Gazette, 1957.

Blom, Frans and Oliver La Farge: *Tribes and Temples: A Record of the Expedition to Middle America Conducted by The Tulane University of Louisiana in 1925*. New Orleans: The Tulane University of Louisiana, 1926.

Blotner, Joseph. *Faulkner: A Biography*. New York: Random House, 1974.

Bradley, James with Ron Powers. *Flags of our Fathers*. New York: Bantam Books, 2000.

Brokaw, Zoanne Sherlock. "Oliver La Farge: His Fictional Navajo." A Thesis Submitted to the Faculty of the Department of English in Partial Fulfillment of the Requirements for the Degree of Master of Arts in the Graduate College, The University of Arizona, 1965.

Caffey, David L., ed. *Yellow Sun, Bright Sky: The Indian Country Stories of Oliver La Farge*. Albuquerque: University of New Mexico Press, 1988.

Chamberlain, John. "Books of the Times". *The New York Times*, 6/15/1934.

Clemens, S. L. *The Adventures of Tom Sawyer*. New York: Three Sirens Press, 1933.

Dew, Charles B. *The Making of a Racist: A Southerner Reflects on Family, History, and the Slave Trade*. Charlottesville and London: University of Virginia Press, 2016.

Dingledine, Raymond C., Jr., Lena Barksdale and Marion Belt Nesbit. *Virginia's History*. New York: Charles Scribner's Sons, 1956.

Erdrich, Louise. *Love Medicine*. New York: Henry Holt and Company, 1984.

_____. *The Round House*. New York: Harper Collins Publishers, 2012.

Faulkner, William. *Mosquitoes*. New York: Liveright, 1997.

Gansworth, Eric. *If I Ever Get Out of Here: A Novel with Paintings*. New York: Scholastic, Inc., 2013

Grandin, Greg, Deborah T. Levenson and Elizabeth Oglesby, eds. *The Guatemala Reader: History, Culture, Politics*. Durham and London: Duke University Press, 2011.

Gwynn, Frederick and Joseph Blotner, eds. *Faulkner in the University: Class Conferences at the University of Virginia, 1957-1958*. Charlottesville: University Press of Virginia, 1959.

Hampl, Patricia. *The Art of the Wasted Day*. New York: Viking, 2018.

Harvey, Robert A. "Oliver La Farge as a Literary Interpreter of Navajo Indian Culture." Submitted to the Department of English, Oklahoma Agricultural and Mechanical College, in Partial Fulfillment of the Requirements for the Degree of Master of Arts, 1949.

Hecht, Robert A. *Oliver La Farge and the American Indian: A Biography*. Metuchen, New Jersey: The Scarecrow Press, Inc., 1991.

Hemphill, William Edwin, Marvin Wilson Schlegal and Sadie Ethel Engleberg. *Cavalier Commonwealth: History and Government of Virginia*. New York: McGraw-Hill Book Company, Inc., 1957.

Hilburn, Robert. *Johnny Cash: The Life*. New York: Little, Brown and Company, 2013.

Hillerman, Tony, ed. *The Spell of New Mexico*. Albuquerque: University of New Mexico Press, 1976.

Hutchison, Percy. "A Novel in Verse by Christopher La Farge". *The New York Times*, 6/17/1934.

Irving, Debby. *Waking Up White and Finding Myself in the Story of Race*. Cambridge, MA: Elephant Room Press, 2014.

Jackson, Helen Hunt. *Ramona*. Boston: Little, Brown and Company, 1884.

Kleinpoppen, Paul. "Some Notes on Oliver La Farge.: University of Nebraska Press: *Studies in American indian Literature*, New Series, Vol. 10, No. 2, Monograph No. 1 (Spring 1986), pp. 69-120.

Krim, Seymour. *you & me*. New York: Holt, Rinehart, and Winston, 1968.

Kupperman, Karen Ordahl. *Pocahontas and the English Boys: Caught Between Cultures in Early Virginia*. New York: New York University Press, 2019.

La Farge, Christopher. *Hoxsie Sells His Acres*. New York: Coward-McCann, Inc., 1934.

La Farge, John Pendaries. *Turn Left at the Sleeping Dog: Scripting the Santa Fe Legend, 1920–1955*. Albuquerque: University of New Mexico Press, 2001.

La Farge, Oliver. *A Pictorial History of the American Indian*. New York: Crown Publishers, Inc., 1956.

_____. *All the Young Men*. Boston and New York: Houghton Mifflin Company, 1935.

_____. *Behind the Mountains*. Cambridge: The Riverside Press, 1951.

_____. *Cochise of Arizona (The Pipe of Peace Is Broken)*. New York: Aladdin Books, 1955.

_____. *The Copper Pot*. Boston: Houghton Mifflin Company, 1942.

_____. *The Enemy Gods*. Boston: Houghton Mifflin Company, 1937.

_____. *Laughing Boy*. Boston: Houghton Mifflin Company, 1929.

_____. *Long Pennant*. Boston: Houghton Mifflin Company, 1933.

_____. *Raw Material*. Boston: Houghton Mifflin Company, 1945.

_____, with the assistance of Arthur N. Morgan. *Santa Fe: The Autobiography of a Southwestern Town*. Norman: University of Oklahoma Press.

_____. *Sparks Fly Upward*. Boston: Houghton Mifflin Company, 1931.

_____, and Douglas Byers. *The Year Bearer's People*. New Orleans: The Department of Middle American Research, The Tulane University of Louisiana, 1931.

La Flesche, Francis. *The Middle Years: Indian Schoolboys of the Omaha Tribe*. Madison: University of Wisconsin Press, 1963.

Lee, Hermione. *Willa Cather: Double Lives*. New York: Pantheon Books, 1989.

McNickle, D'Arcy. *Indian Man: A Life of Oliver La Farge*. Bloomington: Indiana University Press, 1971.

"Oliver La Farge Is Dead at 61; Author Helped Indians' Cause". *The New York Times*, 8/3/1963.

Parsons, Elsie Crews, ed. *American Indian Life*. Lincoln: University of Nebraska Press, 1922.

Miller, Stephen. *Johnny Cash: The Life of an American Icon*. London: Omnibus Press, 2003.

Orange, Tommy. "Native American Heritage Month." *Washington Post*, 11/21/2018.

_____. *There There*. New York: Alfred A. Knopf, 2018.

Pearce, T. M. *Oliver La Farge*. New York: Twayne Publishers, Inc., 1972.

Preston, Douglas. *Talking to the Ground: One Family's Journey on Horseback across the Sacred Land of the Navajo*. New York: Simon & Schuster, 1995.

Railton, Ben. *Contesting the Past, Reconstructing the Nation: American Literature and Culture In the Gilded Age, 1876–1893*. Tuscaloosa: The University of Alabama Press, 2007.

_____. *History and Hope in American Literature: Models of Critical Patriotism*. Lanham, Maryland: Roman and Littlefield, 2017.

Reed, John Shelton. *Dixie Bohemia: A French Quarter Circle in the 1920s*. Baton Rouge: Louisiana State University Press, 2012.

Schulman, Sandra Hale. *Don't Tell Me How I Looked Falling: The Ballad of Peter La Farge*. Slink Productions, 2012.

Scott, Winfield Townley, ed. *The Man with the Calabash Pipe: Some Observations by Oliver La Farge*. Boston: Houghton Mifflin Company, 1966.

Silko, Leslie Marmon. *Ceremony*. New York: Penguin Books, 1977.

Simkins, Francis Butler, Spotswood Hunnicut Jones and Sidman P. Poole. *Virginia: History And Government*. New York: Charles Scribner's Sons, 1957.

Smith, E. Ehrlich. *Our Virginia: A Description of Virginia for Young People*. Richmond: States Publishing Company, 1923.

Smithey, Marvin, "compiler". *Brunswick County, Virginia: Information for the Homeseeker And Investor*. Richmond: Williams Printing Company, 1907.

Springston, Rex. "Happy Slaves? The peculiar story of three Virginia school textbooks." *Richmond Times Dispatch*, 4/14/2018.

Sydenstricker, Edgar and A. I. Burger. *School History of Virginia*. Lynchburg, Virginia: Dulaney-Boatwright Company, 1914.

Treuer, Anton. *Everything You Wanted to Know about Indians But Were Afraid to Ask*. St. Paul, MN: Borealis Books, 2012.

Treuer, David. *The Heartbeat of Wounded Knee: Native America from 1890 to the Present*. New York: Riverhead Books, 2019.

_____. *Native American Fiction: A User's Manual*. St. Paul, MN: Graywolf Press, 2006.

"Trump turns 'Pocahontas' into an insult" (editorial). *Charlottesville Daily Progress*, 10/22/2018.

Twain, Mark. *Roughing It*. *Roughing It* was first published in 1872. This edition was specifically created in 1992 for the Book-of-the Month Club.

Wayland, John W., Ph.D. *A History of Virginia for Boys and Girls*. New York: The MacMillan Company, 1925.

Willis, Carrie Hunter and Lucy S. Saunders. *The Story of Virginia*. New York: Newsom and Company, 1948.

Yarnell, James L. *John La Farge: A Biographical and Critical Study*. Oxfordshire: Routledge Press, 2016.

ABOUT THE AUTHOR

Proal Heartwell lives in Charlottesville, Virginia, where he teaches English at Village School, which he co-founded in 1995. He is the author of *Goronwy and Me: A Narrative of Two Lives* and the novels *Divided We Fall* and *A Game of Catch*. He is also the editor of the books *A Little Off the Top: Stories of Haircuts, Barbers, and Barber Shops* and *One For the Road: An Anthology of Road Trip Writing*.

CPSIA information can be obtained
at www.ICGtesting.com
Printed in the USA
LVHW022115010221
678029LV00016B/588/J

9 780578 804941